ADMINISTRATIVE LAW

Administrative Law

THE INFORMAL PROCESS

By PETER WOLL

UNIVERSITY OF CALIFORNIA PRESS
BERKELEY, LOS ANGELES, LONDON

UNIVERSITY OF CALIFORNIA PRESS
BERKELEY AND LOS ANGELES, CALIFORNIA

UNIVERSITY OF CALIFORNIA PRESS, LTD.
LONDON, ENGLAND

DESIGNED BY WARD RITCHIE
PRINTED IN THE UNITED STATES OF AMERICA

To Mary

Preface

This book is the result of many years of research in the twilight zone of American administrative law, the informal processes of adjudication used by administrative agencies. The beginnings were made at Cornell University under the inspiration of Professor Arch Dotson of the Department of Government, to whom is owed an unqualified debt of major proportions. The excellent law and liberal arts libraries of Cornell, as well as those of UCLA, served to supply raw material, which was later enhanced through interviews with governmental officials at the national level too numerous to mention. Considerable scholarly debt is also owed to Professors Foster II. Sherwood and J. A. C. Grant, of the UCLA Department of Political Science, who have given me encouragement at various stages in the development of this project.

Special thanks are due to the *Cornell Law Quarterly* for permission to reprint in substantially the same form my article entitled "The Development of Shortened Procedure in American Administrative Law" (© 1959 by Cornell University), which appeared in the Fall 1959 issue and forms chapter ii of this work,

All facts and interpretations presented are my sole responsibility. I am a political scientist, not a professional lawyer. A very broad approach is taken to the subject of administrative law and its role in the political and legal system, and at some points this may be at variance with strict legal thinking on these matters. Nevertheless, although possibly contentious, it is hoped that this book will serve a particularly useful purpose in getting new information before those interested. The implications of informal administrative procedure, which does not fit the legal pattern, are of particular concern in an age that may be characterized more by computer adjudication than by traditional adversary proceedings.

PETER WOLL

Los Angeles, California
August 21, 1962

vii

Contents

Introduction

There is little doubt in the minds of most that the growth of and present position occupied by administrative agencies presents problems of magnitude to students of the law and of government. Individuals, in their daily lives, come into contact directly or indirectly with such agencies twenty-four hours a day. The administrative process not only affects individuals but also shapes the relationships among governmental departments in a way entirely beyond prediction by those who devised our structure of government.

Under our original scheme of government there was to be a "separation of powers," which, although it permitted the intermixture of functions to some extent among departments, was nevertheless designed to guarantee that each department would retain the primary function assigned to it. Thus Congress was to be the primary legislative authority, the judiciary the judicial authority, and the Presidency was to retain primary control over the execution of the law. Of course, in order to ensure such a system each department had to be given the means of self-protection, the weapons consisting of specific powers falling within the jurisdiction of adversary departments. This original system was designed to effect the constitutionalist's ideal of limited government. Democracy, insofar as it was to be practiced at all, was to be severely limited.

With the rise of the administrative branch many serious questions have been posed both for constitutional government and for the more newly created democratic norms of our society. Constitutional government requires limitation through counterbalancing the departments and through the requirement that governmental agencies act in accordance with traditional legal rights protected by the Constitution. Democratic government requires participation by the people in the formulation of public policy. There is no provision in the Constitution designed to control administrative agencies, and the very ambiguities of the Constitution permit Congress to create a "headless fourth branch,"

1

the independent regulatory commissions. The constitutional limitations, then, which are operative with respect to the three traditional branches of government do not control the activities of administrative agencies.

Regulatory agencies are principally engaged in rule-making and adjudication; thus they combine, under the auspices of one agency although in separate divisions of such agencies, legislative and judicial functions which we can infer the Constitution intended to keep in separate departments of government.[1] This book is concerned with the adjudicative functions of administrative agencies, which are of particular importance in that through adjudication general rules are given concrete application in individual cases. It is frequently through adjudication that public policy, formulated through administrative rule-making or by Congress, is implemented. Adjudication is primarily procedural in nature, although substantive rules are of critical importance in shaping the final result of an adjudicative proceeding.

The hypothesis which this book is going to investigate is that requirements of public policy, *expertise,* and speed have rendered administrative adjudication today primarily informal in nature. Adjudication will be defined broadly. John Dickinson has pointed out that "what distinguishes legislation from adjudication is that the former affects the rights of individuals in the abstract and must be applied in a further proceeding before the legal position of any particular individual will be definitely touched by it; while adjudication operates concretely upon individuals in their individual capacity." [2] Generally speaking, adjudication involves an adversary proceeding in which a final determination is made. The term "adversary" does not require in the general sense articulated conflict among parties, but rather an asserted claim on the part of a specific party requiring a determination according to legal standards.

The question which naturally arises is what is the significance of informal administrative adjudication? In order to answer this it will be necessary to discuss the development of administrative law and the role of administrative agencies within our legal system. This discussion will preface the main body of this work, which will present evidence with regard to the hypothesis noted above.

Finally, because the scope of the administrative process precludes an examination of all agencies exercising adjudicative powers, concentration has been placed upon some of the more significant and characteristic agencies. These are: (1) the Interstate Commerce Commission (ICC); (2) the Federal Communications Commission (FCC); (3) the Securities and Exchange Commission (SEC); (4) the Federal Trade Commission (FTC); (5) the Civil Aeronautics Board (CAB); (6) the National Labor Relations Board (NLRB); (7) the Internal Revenue Service (IRS); (8) the Veterans Administration (VA); and finally (9) the Bureau of Old-Age and Survivors Insurance within the Social Security Administration. From an examination of these characteristic agencies an accurate composite picture of the administrative process may be gained, and valid generalizations advanced.

Chapter I

ADMINISTRATION, THE CONSTITUTION, AND THE COMMON LAW

The rise of the administrative process parallels the development of the United States into a large, complex, and industrialized nation. Requirements of *expertise* have necessitated specialization resulting in the development of administrative agencies. Increasingly, public policy has required continuity, which in turn has strengthened the administrative process, the only governmental branch capable of lending continuity to policy. Congress, faced with an increased workload and the technical nature of much modern legislation, has relied upon administrative agencies for advice. With the development of economic regulation it was the administrative branch which was placed squarely in the center of activity, particularly as it became evident that neither Congress nor the judicial system could handle their respective functions adequately in the regulatory realm. This is not to say that administrative agencies usurped the functions of coördinate departments; quite the contrary is the case. Both Congress and the judiciary have voluntarily relinquished power and permitted the broad exercise of discretion on the part of administrators; otherwise the administrative process could not function as it does today. At the national level Congress, and at the state level state legislatures, have been particularly instrumental not only in delegating their own powers to administrative agencies, but also in placing judicial power in the hands of such agencies. Administrative adjudication developed both because of these general considerations and because of the inadequacies of the courts in a number of categories.

The first failing of the courts was their inability to specialize. Regulatory adjudication requires *expertise* in a narrowly defined area. The courts were not equipped, either in terms of personnel or function, to handle such adjudication. Although in the eighteenth and early nineteenth centuries courts in some instances had jurisdiction over the establishment of tolls on public roads, thus giving them a rate-making function, it was clear that jurisdiction of this type could not be extended into more advanced areas of economic regulation. To the individual trained in the traditional legal manner, adjudication is an area of *expertise* per se; thus, any judge should be able to handle any instance of adjudication, regardless of subject matter. Indeed, as will be pointed out later, one of the principal suppositions of the common law is that only those trained in the law should have judicial power. On the other hand, the modern administrator tends to consider adjudication a function both of *expertise* in the particular subject-matter area involved and of *policy* considerations. The judge will make his decision based upon evidence introduced according to procedures acceptable in the common law; the administrator will not only be concerned with common-law considerations, but will also take into account public policy, the public interest, and the effect of the decision in securing proper regulation.

Second, the judicial branch is placed in the position of an umpire, adjudicating only those disputes properly brought to it for consideration and rendering decisions only on the basis of evidence introduced as such during the course of the proceeding. True, in certain instances judicial notice may be taken of facts beyond the record, but strictly speaking the court is to base its decision upon the record developed by the litigants during the course of the proceeding. Of course the judge may also choose whatever premise he wishes, without particular regard to the record, and generally the courts exercise substantial discretionary power, becoming in fact instruments of policy, although strictly speaking this should not be the case. Regardless of the informal discretion judges possess, their umpire status does not give them the degree of flexibility necessary in the modern regulatory realm. Too often, in modern regulation, effectiveness is secured only through the ability to *initiate* action, and the passive nature of the judicial branch renders it ineffective in this sense. The judge does not possess the legal flexibility, the staff, or the funds to conduct investigations into particular areas; however, such investigation is frequently necessary to adjudicate numerous classes of cases arising before administrative tribunals. Administrative agencies have been established to protect the public interest, and they do this by becoming a party to disputes within their jurisdiction. They represent the general public in opposition to particular private parties against whom they have found evidence suggesting possible legal violation. In this way the administrative agency assumes the legal burden that under the common law would have to rest upon a private party. Expense and the possibility of economic sanction normally prevent private parties from joining in combat with those whom they suspect of violating regulatory statutes or regulations. For this reason the names of complainants remain confidential before many agencies.

A third judicial inadequacy is the inability of the court system, as presently constituted, to handle the large volume of cases which necessarily arise under modern economic and social legislation. For example, in any one year the Veterans Administration adjudicates in its formal procedural realm (the Board of Veterans Appeals) almost half the number of cases adjudicated by the entire federal court system. But informal adjudication handled by the VA in a year amounts to more than thirty times the number of cases adjudicated by the federal court system. Administrative agencies are able to adjudicate a large volume of cases because they utilize informal adjudicative techniques and rely upon the institutional decision-making process. Common-law courts cannot utilize either of these devices as effectively.

A final judicial problem associated with the rise of the administrative process has been judicial hostility to legislative purposes at all levels of government, with respect to social and economic legislation. The courts have traditionally been conservative and basically opposed to the ends of such legislation. Through control over the disposition of cases arising under such statutes the judiciary was able to frustrate the goals of the legislature; therefore, legislatures have increasingly placed these areas of adjudication beyond the initial purview of the courts. This is illustrated by early workmen's compensation laws, and later by the creation of the Federal Trade Commission which purposely was given powers independent of the judiciary, the latter having interpreted the Sherman Act in a way that resulted in weak antitrust and antimonopoly regulation.

In summary, the rise of the administrative process, coupling legislative and adjudicative powers, was necessitated by: (1)

the development of an industrialized and complex society requiring economic regulation; (2) the need for specialization to develop the necessary *expertise,* flexible regulation to parallel the changing needs of the regulated field, and continuity of public policy; and (3) the evident inability of the judicial process to perform the necessary adjudication with regard to the vastly expanded scope of governmental activity. The excessive formalism and prejudices of the common law could not be adapted to the changing needs of society. Administrative law, like equity, developed to meet a common-law deficiency; but unlike equity it completely removed a significant area of adjudication from judicial control.

What has been the reaction of the legal profession and the courts to this development?

CONSTITUTIONAL AND COMMON-LAW FRAMEWORK

The fact of administrative adjudication appears to conflict with both the common law and the Constitution. Article III requires that the judicial power of the United States "shall be vested in one Supreme Court, and in such inferior courts as the Congress may from time to time ordain and establish." [1] The courts, however, have constitutionally justified the exercise of judicial functions by extrajudicial agencies by distinguishing between (1) the judicial power of the United States under Article III of the Constitution and (2) judicial power in the generic sense. The courts will permit the exercise of general judicial functions outside of the judicial branch; thus administrative adjudication is permitted by constitutional doctrine. On the other hand, when the judicial power of the United States, under Article III, can be identified, the courts require its vestment in the Supreme Court, or in the inferior courts established by Congress. Conversely, judicial power which is not encompassed by Article III cannot generally be vested in the judicial branch. [2] Judicial functions may be vested in administrative agencies at both the national and state level, and if necessary they may be united with legislative functions. [3]

Finality is a necessary attribute of judicial power, which with respect to specific parties involves the determination of liabilities, on the basis of law or rules in existence. Final judicial power may reside outside of the judicial branch. The Supreme Court has stated

> we do not consider Congress can either withdraw from judicial cognizance any matter which, from its nature, is the subject of a suit at the common law, or in equity, or admiralty; nor, on the other hand, can it bring under the judicial power a matter which, from its nature, is not a subject for judicial determination. At the same time there are matters, involving public rights, which may be presented in such form that the judicial power is capable of acting on them, and which are susceptible of judicial determination, but which Congress may or may not bring within the cognizance of the courts of the United States, as it may deem proper.[4]

Judicial finality may, then, be vested in administrative agencies, provided the courts do not find reason for intervention. Such finality is *de facto,* not *de jure.* It results from judicial self-restraint, not legal prohibitions upon judicial review. There is little doubt that where the courts want to intervene they can find sufficient legal reason for so doing. Long-standing criteria precluding such review, for example, judicial refusal to review issues of "fact" (*expertise*), as opposed to those of "law," may be ignored if the courts decide that intervention is necessary. In certain cases, where final judicial power is given by Congress to an administrative agency, the courts have refused to intervene. In others, regardless of apparent congressional intent to limit justifications for review, the courts have intervened to prevent denial of due process of law, thus using a constitutional criterion which takes precedence over statutory standards.

One notable scholar has concluded, with regard to the problem of giving judicial functions to extrajudicial agencies:

> . . . though the courts will not perform administrative acts, there is no *constitutional* objection to vesting the performance of acts essentially judicial in character in the hands of the executive or administrative agents, provided the performance of these functions is properly incidental to the execution by the department in question of functions peculiarly its own. Furthermore . . . there is . . . subject to the same qualification, no objection to rendering the administra-

tive determinations conclusive, that is, without appeal to the courts, provided in general the requirements of due process of law as regards the right of the person affected to a hearing, to produce evidence, etc., have been met.[5]
This statement is accurate today, although the requirements of due process have changed. Generally, due process requires administrative adherence to the judicial model, insofar as feasible; however, because of the unique needs of administrative adjudication, the courts have permitted administrative practices which would not be acceptable in a court of law.

The Common Law and Administrative Adjudication

Although there is apparently no constitutional problem arising from administrative agencies' exercise of conclusive jurisdiction over matters of a judicial nature, there is a common-law objection to any exercise of judicial functions outside the realm of the ordinary court system. A fundamental common-law concept is that of "supremacy of law." One of the best early expressions of this theory is found in Coke's *Institutes*. In speaking of the jurisdiction of the Court of Kings Bench he noted

. . . this court hath not only jurisdiction to correct errors in judicial proceeding, but other errors and misdemeanors extrajudicial tending to the breach of the peace, or oppression of the subjects, or raising of faction, controversy, debate, or any other manner of misgovernment; so that no wrong or injury, either public or private, can be done, but that this shall be reformed or punished in one court or other by due course of law.[6]

Perhaps the best known articulation of the doctrine of rule (or supremacy) of law is found in the writings of Dicey. In his classic *Introduction to the Study of the Law of the Constitution* he distinguishes three characteristics of the supremacy of law, or, as he termed this concept, the rule of law.

First, "no man is punishable or can be lawfully made to suffer in body or goods except for a distinct breach of law established in the ordinary legal manner before the ordinary courts of the land."[7] In Dicey's terms the "ordinary courts" are the common-law courts and "the ordinary legal manner" refers to common-law procedure.

Second, the rule of law means "not only that with us no man is above the law, but (what is a different thing) that here every man, whatever be his rank or condition, is subject to the ordinary law of the realm and amenable to the jurisdiction of the ordinary tribunals." [8] Here Dicey refers to his belief that under the rule of law governmental officials must be subject to common-law jurisdiction.

Third, "we may say that the constitution is pervaded by the rule of law on the ground that the general principles of the constitution (as for example the right to personal liberty . . .) are with us the result of judicial decisions determining the rights of private persons in particular cases brought before the Courts; whereas under many foreign constitutions the security (such as it is) given to the rights of individuals results, or appears to result, from the general principles of the constitution." [9] In brief, "our constitution . . . is a judge-made constitution, and it bears on its face all the features, good or bad, of judge-made law." [10]

In order for Dicey's common-law concept of the rule of law to be realized it is necessary that adjudication between the government and private parties be placed within the jurisdiction of common-law courts. Further, government agencies must be subject to common-law jurisdiction, as no one is above the law. Dicey was attacking, of course, *droit administratif*, although in the beginning of the twentieth century he recognized that in England administrative law was developing which, although not like *droit administratif*, was nevertheless separate from the common law. In his introduction to the eighth edition of *Law of the Constitution* he reiterated an opinion previously expressed in article form:[11]

Recent Acts have given judicial or quasi-judicial authority to officials who stand more or less in connection with, and therefore may be influenced by, the government of the day, and hence have in some cases excluded, and in others indirectly diminished, the authority of the law Courts. . . . It must . . . be noted that the *invasion* of the rule of law by imposing judicial functions upon officials is due, in part, to the whole current of legislative opinion in favor of extending the sphere of the State's authority.[12]

Why have common-law theorists insisted that judicial power

reside in the hands of the courts? Primarily because they felt that only those trained in the law should administer it. In the United States, Roscoe Pound was the most articulate spokesman for the legal profession in opposition to the rise of administrative adjudication. Pound, in 1914, characterized administrative adjudication (or what he termed "executive justice") as "one of those reversions to justice without law." [13] He noted, for example, "workmen's compensation legislation is threatening to take a great mass of tort litigation out of the domain of *law* and confide it to *administration*." [14] To Pound, administration, or administrative adjudication, was the antithesis of law.

Pound sensed the crisis developing in the common law at the beginning of the twentieth century:

> The experience of the past indicates that if we improve the output of judicial justice till the adjustment of human relations by our courts is brought into better accord with the moral sense of the public at large and is achieved without unreasonable, not to say prohibitive delay and expense, the onward march of executive justice will soon cease. But we must be vigilant. Legislatures are pouring out an ever-increasing volume of laws. The old judicial machinery has been found inadequate to enforce them. They touch the most vital interests of the community, and it demands enforcement. Hence the executive is turned to. Summary administrative action becomes the fashion. An elective judiciary, sensitive to the public will, yields up its prerogatives, and the return to a government of men is achieved. If we are to be spared a season of oriental justice, if we are to preserve the common-law doctrine of supremacy of law, the profession and the courts must take up vigorously and fearlessly the problem of today—how to *administer* the law to meet the demands of the world that is.[15]

Here Pound notes that one of the reasons for the rise of administrative law is judicial inadequacy; however, he was unable to foresee the vast expansion of the administrative branch, for reasons apart from judicial inadequacy, that rendered impossible any attempt to reshape the judiciary for the purpose of absorbing adjudicative areas concomitant with administrative expansion.

Further, it should be noted that Pound refers to the subversion of the supremacy of law as the central problem of administrative law.

Pound goes on to state that the advantages claimed for executive justice "are those which are claimed for justice without law; directness, expedition, conformity to the popular will for the time being, freedom from the bonds of purely traditional rules, freedom from technical rules of evidence and power to act upon the everyday instincts of ordinary men."[16] Executive justice, however, "is an evil, even if sometimes a necessary evil. It has always been and in the long run it always will be crude and as variable as the personalities of officials. No one can long be suffered to wield the royal power of deciding without fixed principles according to convictions of right but one trained to subordinate impulse and will to reason, disciplined in the exercise of reason and experienced in the difficult art of deciding controversies."[17]

What are the advantages of judicial justice, which is to say adjudication by the common-law courts? First, "with respect both to the law-declaring and to the deciding function, it combines the possibilities of certainty and of flexibility better than any other form of administering justice. It provides for certainty through the training of the judge in logical development and systematic exposition of legal principles. It provides for growth by permitting a scientific testing of principles with reference to concrete causes and correction of rules through experience of their application and a gradual process of inclusion and exclusion upon rational principles."[18]

In the second place, there are limitations upon arbitrary action by judges which do not operate with respect to administrative officials. These checks are: "(1) The judge, from his very training, is impelled to conform his action to certain, known standards. Professional habit leads him in every case to seek such standards before acting and to refer his action thereto. (2) Every decision is subject to criticism by a learned profession, to whose opinion the judge, as a member of the profession, is keenly sensitive. (3) Every decision and the case on which it was based, appear in full in public records."[19] It is evident from an examination of the first two checks, operative with regard to judges, that Pound relies upon the characteristics of the legal profession to ensure responsible adjudication on the part of the judge.

In 1921 Pound published *The Spirit of the Common Law*,[20] in which he further clarified the reasons for common-law opposition to administrative adjudication. He noted that the common law "succeeds everywhere in molding rules, whatever their origin, into accord with its principles and in maintaining those principles in the face of formidable attempts to overthrow or to supersede them."[21] Further, "we assume that our common-law notions are part of the legal order of nature and are unable to understand that any reasonable being can harbor legal conceptions that run counter to them, and the Anglo-Saxon refuses to be ruled by any other law."[22]

Pound felt that the ascendency of administrative law in the twentieth century has its parallel in the similar domination in the sixteenth century of the common law by executive courts, such as the King's Council, the Star Chamber, the Court of Requests, and the Court of Chancery.[23] In the sixteenth century, "in place of the magistrate limited by law and held to walk strictly in the paths fixed by the custom of the realm, men sought to set up a benevolent guardian of social interests who should have power to do freely whatever in his judgment protection of those interests might involve; in place of deliberate judicial tribunals, *restrained by formal procedure and deciding according to fixed principles,* they turned to *offhand administrative tribunals* in which the relations of individuals with each other and with the state were adjusted summarily according to the notions for the time being of an administrative officer as to what the general interest or good conscience demanded, unencumbered by many rules."[24] The common-law judiciary defeated administrative absolutism, and "it became a doctrine that it was the function of the common law and of common-law courts to stand between the individual and oppressive action by the state. . . ."[25]

The doctrine of the supremacy of law requires that public service may not "be left to the arbitrary will of those who perform it. In each case the social interest in general security requires that it be guided and regulated by reason."[26] Reason is a monopoly of the judiciary, in matters of law. Common-law doctrine "assumes that experience will afford the most satisfactory foundation for standards of action and principles of decision. It holds that law is not to be made arbitrarily by a fiat of the sovereign will, but is to be discovered by judicial and juristic experience of the rules and principles which in the past have accomplished or have failed to accomplish justice. Where such doctrine obtains, not merely the interpretation and application of legal rules but in large measure the ascertainment of them must be left to the disciplined reason of the judges. . . ."[27]

Although Pound's ideas may seem outdated today, they nevertheless represent an important segment of thought in the American Bar Association; consequently they have had a profound influence upon attempts by that organization to control administrative law. Pound is expressing what are frequently the inarticulate premises of those seeking stricter statutory control over administrative adjudication.

Attempts to Control Administrative Adjudication

In 1927 Dickinson pointed out that

In so far as administrative adjudication is coming in certain fields to take the place of adjudication by law courts, the supremacy of law as formulated in Dicey's first proposition is overridden. But a possible way of escaping this result is left open by his second proposition. An administrative determination is an act of a governmental officer or officers; and if it be true that all the acts of such officers are subject to be questioned in the courts, it is then possible to have the issue of any questionable administrative adjudication raised and decided anew in a law court, with the special advantages and guaranties of the procedure at law. We here see the reason why the question of court review of administrative determinations has come to be of such central importance and has been the focus of so much discussion since the rise of the administrative procedure. For just in so far as administrative determinations are subject to court review, a means exists for maintaining the supremacy of law, though at one remove and as a sort of secondary line of defence.[28]

Dickinson accurately concludes that "administrative justice exists in defiance of the supremacy of law only insofar as administrative adjudications are final or conclusive, and not subject to correction by a law court. To some undefined extent, however, they are final, and there seems to be a tendency at work to make them increasingly so." [29]

By the beginning of the New Deal it became evident to the American Bar Association and certain elements in the judiciary that something had to be done if the judiciary was not to lose a significant portion of its power to the fast-growing administrative process. Dicey's concept that cases and controversies should be decided *initially* by the common-law courts was obviously not an appropriate proposal in light of the exigencies of the times. Further, as early as the late twenties it became evident to some that judicial review was not an entirely realistic device to control administrative action. Lacking the ability to put into effect these two remedies, the American Bar Association decided that the best course of action was to render the administrative process as similar to the judicial process of the courts, in a procedural sense, as possible. Legal theorists developed the idea that the supremacy of law could in effect be maintained if these new agencies, although they were not and possibly could not be courts in the true common-law sense of that word, were nevertheless made to act like courts.

In discussing the American Bar Association it is of the utmost importance to remember that this group contains many diverse strands of thought, and although it frequently takes official stands on particular issues, these views do not represent those of all the membership. It is a mistake of great magnitude to assume conformity of attitude among the legal profession. Compared with other groups, there is generally a greater awareness of the legal aspects of particular problems among lawyers, and perhaps a greater respect for procedural protections in adjudication; beyond this there are sharp contrasts in the group. Nevertheless, during the early part of the New Deal, as administrative agencies were created with a degree of rapidity that astounded many, the American Bar Association did take an official stand in relation to the control of administrative law, and it was later instrumental in securing the passage of legislation for this purpose. Many lawyers, of course, who worked for both new and old administrative agencies took positions in sharp opposition to the position of the

American Bar Association. This tendency toward diversity within the ABA, between government and private lawyers, increased as the agencies became more highly developed. Today, the views of many agency lawyers are in sharp opposition to the official ABA position, and there are other diverse points of view represented within the Association. It is important to remember, in the discussion that follows, that in dealing with the ABA it is the *official* stand of the group that is most often being described and analyzed.

The American Bar Association established a Committee on Administrative Law in May of 1933, and the first report of this committee contains the seeds of future ABA proposals for the control of administrative adjudication. The committee noted:

> When . . . the administrative official exercises a quasi-judicial function, he may be expected to conform to the sort of procedure which *has been found best adapted* to the determination of the rights and obligations of the individual in his controversies with other individuals and with the Government. Certain fundamental safeguards of notice, opportunity for hearing, and determination or review of issues of fact and of law by an independent tribunal (and eventually, on questions of law at least, by a court) are involved, and, indeed, are necessary if justice is to be done to the individual.[30]

In the view of this committee those procedures which have been found best adapted to the realization of justice are common-law procedures; thus common-law due process was to be transferred to the administrative process. The desire of the legal profession to force the administrative process to conform to certain formal judicial procedures is evident from the very beginning.

In 1934 the American Bar Association took another tack and the Special Committee on Administrative Law recommended the abolition of independent boards and commissions and the establishment of an administrative court system.[31] This proposal was destined to be repeated at relatively frequent intervals by various groups, between 1934 and 1960. The most notable instances of such proposals were by the President's Committee on Administrative Management, in 1937, and by the Hoover Commission, in 1955. Later proposals followed the basic design of the original, which hoped to segregate judicial functions and transfer executive and legislative functions to appropriate departments. To some extent this was a return to the basic constitutional model, with the thought that a stricter separation of powers should be maintained. The bulk of administrative adjudication was to be handled, if not by a common-law court, at least by an administrative court which would be more like an "ordinary" court in appearance than the typical regulatory agency which combines all three functions of government.

Just as proposals for administrative courts were destined to be made, they were destined to fail. With regard to the first proposal, some elements in the Bar Association thought the proposed administrative court smacked too much of the French system. They did not want a Continental system in America, as it offended the basic common-law supremacy of law doctrine. In this respect Dicey apparently still had influence in shaping the folklore of the American legal profession.[32] Failing in their attempts to institute administrative courts, the Special Committee reverted to its original scheme and proposed legislation for stricter procedural control over administrative agencies. In this spirit the Walter-Logan bill, similar in most details to a special ABA administrative law bill, was supported by the ABA and passed by both houses of Congress; however, Roosevelt vetoed the bill in 1940, and Congress was unable to override.[33]

The Walter-Logan Bill

The Walter-Logan bill provides an interesting example of the extent to which the legal profession was willing to go in forcing the administrative process into a judicial mold. With respect to the rule-making (legislative) functions of administrative agencies, the bill provided that "hereafter administrative rules and all amendments or modifications or supplements of existing rules implementing or filling in the details of any statute affecting the rights of persons or property shall be issued . . . only after publication of notice and public hearings." [34] In addition to this extreme provision regarding rule-making, the bill provided that any "substantially interested" person could, within a three-year period, petition the agency for a reconsideration of any rule, and could furthermore demand a hearing. In this manner the bill attempted to enforce common-law due process, applicable only to adjudication, upon the *legislative* process of administrative agencies. It would have been equally appropriate to enforce judicial procedure upon Congress!

With regard to administrative adjudication, the Walter-Logan bill provided for the establishment of intra-agency boards in single-headed agencies, consisting of three employees of the agency, at least one of whom was to be a lawyer. Where practicable, these boards were to hear controversies under the jurisdiction of the agency. Prosecuting and adjudicative functions were to be separated. Opportunity for a hearing before such a board was to be given by the agency concerned to any person aggrieved by an agency decision. Such a hearing was to be judicial in character. With regard to independent agencies (multiple-headed) an examiner was to be permitted to hear controversies in the first instance, but a written record, with findings of fact, and other judicial procedures, were required. At the request of the private party a public hearing before not less than three members of the agency was to be held. If the board had less than three members it was to be designated as single-headed, and the intra-agency board procedure was to be followed. Finally, the bill provided for judicial review of law and fact with regard to *all agency decisions*.

The Walter-Logan bill represents an extreme attempt on the part of the legal profession to judicialize administrative procedure. It was designed to prescribe standard procedure, regardless of statutory provisions specifically shaping the procedures of particular agencies in accordance with their duties and the general character of their jobs. There is a notable contrast, in this regard, with the more flexible provisions of the Administrative Procedure Act of 1946. Furthermore, the sweeping provisions of the bill relating to judicial review gave to the courts powers of review which they could not properly fulfill. The courts themselves have exercised judicial restraint with regard to reviewing the expert determinations of administrative agencies, for they are not equipped to handle the large volume of cases that would arise under their jurisdiction if they were to adopt broad standards under which appeal could be taken to the courts. Also, the Walter-Logan bill overlooked the fact that many administrative determinations are excluded from the purview of the courts by law. The effect of the bill would have been to make *any* administrative decision reviewable by the courts. The bill was a direct outgrowth of the common-law insistence upon the supremacy of law, and upon the right of the citizen to appeal to the "ordinary" courts of the land government actions which purportedly violate constitutional or legal rights. Insofar as cases would not be appealed, the bill attempted to safeguard the citizen by remaking the administrative process in the judicial image.

The Administrative Procedure Act of 1946

After the failure of the Walter-Logan bill, the American Bar Association managed to secure the passage of the Administrative Procedure Act of 1946. This act differed materially from the Walter-Logan bill in that it attempted to regulate administrative procedure while taking into account the requirements of administrative flexibility. The APA of 1946 did not simply extend a blanket requirement for administrative hearings in all cases involving rule-making and adjudication; rather it attempted to distinguish among various types of rules and it called for formal adjudicative procedure only in cases where a hearing was required by statute.[35] This applied both to rule-making and to adjudication. Judicial review was provided "except so far as (1) statutes preclude judicial review or (2) agency action is by law committed to agency discretion."[36] Within the terms of these limitations fairly comprehensive provisions, both for formal hearings and for judicial review, were included in the act.

Other outstanding features of the APA were: (1) requirements for public information (§ 3); (2) establishment of a semi-independent class of hearing examiners (§ 11); (3) requirements for a separation of adjudicative and prosecuting functions within each agency (§ 5); and finally (4) provisions guaranteeing certain procedural protections to private parties subject to administrative jurisdiction.

The effect of the APA is equivocal. Widely hailed as the most important enactment of the century in administrative law, the pre-ABA and post-ABA operations of administrative agencies do not differ from each other significantly. The most important change has been with regard to the position of hearing examiners. Although the provisions regarding the independence of hearing examiners may not be strictly observed in all cases,[37] there is little doubt in the minds of those who deal with the various commissions that the examiners are independent and not subject to the whims of the commissioners. This alone is an important achievement. The separation of functions must be based upon an independent class of hearing officers; once such independence has been destroyed, the prosecuting arm of the agency can easily influence adjudicative decisions.

Further, as a result of the APA, regulations of administrative agencies are now more available to the public, especially in the procedural area. Finally, in the area of judicial review, the scope of review has been significantly broadened by the requirement that in reviewing a case "the court shall review the whole record or such portions thereof as may be cited by any party." This changed the previous rule that a court had to consider only the pro arguments, to determine whether or not there was substantial evidence in favor of the agency. A significant number of cases have reversed the decisions of administrative agencies on this basis.

It should be noted that whereas the Walter-Logan bill attempted to formalize the entire administrative process, the provisions of the APA applied primarily to the *formal administrative process*, the area where hearings are required by statute, or, more rarely, by agency rule. Thus the former bill attempted to require hearings in all cases of adjudication and rule-making; the latter was designed to guarantee minimum procedural safeguards, if the agency already was required to hold a hearing on the basis of other law or regulation.

DUE PROCESS OF LAW IN ADMINISTRATIVE PROCEEDINGS

From the foregoing, it is evident that the primary concern of the American legal profession and the judiciary has been to establish a meaningful concept of due process of law with reference to administrative proceedings, thereby protecting the citizen under the jurisdiction of administrative agencies. The various bills proposed by the American Bar Association have attempted to implement certain criteria of due process in administrative law. This has also been the over-all aim of the judiciary, which, in investigating the "law" of a particular case, attempts to determine (among other things) whether or not procedural due process has been followed.

Generally speaking, due process of law in administration requires that fundamental procedures such as notice, hearing, adequate record, and appeal be maintained. These procedures are formal and are characteristic of the formal stage of administrative adjudication in theory. As presently defined, in order for due process to be operative in administrative proceedings, private parties must have opportunity for recourse to the formal hearing stage within the agency, for only at that stage are procedures sufficiently formalized and opportunity present for further appeal to the judicial branch. Unfortunately, aside from these general observations, it is impossible to define with any degree of precision standards of due process in administrative law. The District of Columbia Court of Appeals noted in the 1942 case of *NBC* v. *FCC:* "Nor has it been made clear by judicial decision what constitutes a minimum compliance with due process in the way of administrative hearing. Presumably this will vary to a considerable extent with the nature of the substantive right, the character and complexity of the issues, the kinds of evidence and factual material, the particular body or official, and the administrative functions involved in the hearing." [38] Although the Administrative Procedure Act was designed to remedy this situation, the indefiniteness of standards of due process remains today.

Common-law procedures which were later to be identified with procedural due process were developed initially to ensure the accurate establishment of the *facts* of a case under adjudication.[39] Disputes were between individuals acting in their private capacities, and fair adjudication was dependent upon the clear articulation and ascertainment of relevant facts which, when established and applied within the proper legal framework, would result in justice being rendered. At a later stage legal procedure came to be thought of not only as a mechanical device for determining fact, but also as a safeguard against arbitrary judgments by *public* officials who were controlled because they operated under the law of the land and could not act in a manner

contrary to that law. Common-law devices for the establishment
of facts, then, insofar as they become associated with due process
of law, may serve the corollary function of bringing government
under the law of the land and thereby protect citizens against
arbitrary exercise of power. As noted above, this latter aspect of
legal procedure is uppermost in the minds of men such as Roscoe
Pound, and therefore has found its way into the literature of
American administrative law.

In the development of the common law the courts have decided that although due process does not necessarily mean judicial process,[40] fundamental judicial procedures of *notice* and
hearing should be preserved. Such hearings must provide, theoretically, the opportunity for the utilization of formal legal procedure, such as oral cross-examination in some instances. Generally speaking common law theorists hold that the more formal
the procedure the better the opportunity for justice. To illustrate
this point consider the reasoning of the Court in *ICC* v. *Louisville
& Nashville Ry. Co.*[41] in which, although a hearing was granted,
it was not considered adequate:

> But the statute gave the right to a full hearing, and that
> conferred the privilege of introducing testimony, and at the
> same time imposed the duty of deciding in accordance with
> the facts proved. A finding without evidence is arbitrary and
> baseless. And if the Government's contention is correct, it
> would mean that the Commission had a power possessed by
> no other officer, administrative body, or tribunal under our
> Government. It would mean that where rights depended
> upon facts, the Commission could disregard all rules of evi-
> dence, and capriciously make findings by administrative fiat.
> Such authority, however beneficently exercised in one case,
> could be injuriously exerted in another; is inconsistent with
> rational justice, and comes under the Constitution's con-
> demnation of all arbitrary exercise of power.

In the comparatively few cases in which such questions
have arisen it has been distinctly recognized that administrative orders, quasi-judicial in character, are void if a hearing
was denied; if that granted was inadequate or manifestly
unfair; if the finding was contrary to the "indisputable character of the evidence." [42]

In *Southern Ry. Co. v. Va.*[43] the Court stated emphatically that a state statute authorizing an administrative officer to require railroads to substitute overhead crossings for existing grade crossings whenever it seemed necessary for the public safety and convenience violated the Fourteenth Amendment because of its failure to provide for notice and hearing. The Court noted that "before its property can be taken under the edict of an administrative officer the appellant is entitled to a fair hearing upon the fundamental facts." [44]

Ideally, then, notice and hearing have traditionally been considered necessary components to due process in administrative proceedings; however, under varying circumstances, administrative exigencies have necessitated judicial recognition of other forms of procedure, although the courts are never happy with the elimination of formal procedure. As a minimum, the courts feel that parties should have an opportunity for a hearing, with the right to present evidence, and so on, at least once in the process of adjudication; theoretically the courts should have the last say through judicial review.

THE DEVELOPMENT OF INFORMAL ADMINISTRATIVE ADJUDICATION

Regardless of the importance of hearings within our legal framework administrative agencies have utilized informal procedure from the very beginning. Although hearings are used in the informal sense, they are entirely different from the type of hearings the judiciary and the legal profession would like to see used, which would more closely approximate judicial hearings. President Roosevelt noted in his veto message, after rejecting the Walter-Logan bill, that

. . . The promotion of expeditious, orderly, and sensible procedure in the conduct of public affairs is a purpose which commends itself not only to the Congress and the courts but to the executive departments and administrative agencies themselves.

I am convinced . . . that in reality the effect of this bill would be to reverse and, to a large extent, cancel one of the most significant and useful trends of the twentieth century in legal administration.

That movement has its origin in the recognition even by the courts themselves that the conventional processes of the courts are not adapted to handling controversies in the mass. Court procedure is adapted to the intensive investigation of individual controversies. But it is impossible to subject the daily routine of fact-finding in many of our agencies to court procedure. Litigation has become costly beyond the ability of the average person to bear. Its technical rules of procedure are often traps for the unwary and technical rules of evidence often prevent common-sense determinations on information which would be regarded as adequate for any business decision. . . . All laymen and most lawyers recognize the inappropriateness of entrusting routine processes of government to the outcome of neverending lawsuits.

The administrative tribunal or agency has been evolved in order to handle controversies arising under particular statutes. It is characteristic of these tribunals that simple and nontechnical hearings take the place of court trials, and informal proceedings supersede rigid and formal pleadings and processes. . . .

Substantial justice remains a higher aim for our civilization than technical legalism. . . .[45]

The Attorney General's Committee on Administrative Procedure was the first and last important study group to recognize the importance of informal adjudication performed by administrative agencies. Its staff was under the direction of Walter Gellhorn, one of the most prominent scholars of administrative law in the country, and included Kenneth Culp Davis, a leading and distinguished scholar in this field. This staff noted that "informal procedures constitute the vast bulk of administrative adjudication and are truly the life blood of the administrative process. No study of administrative procedure can be adequate if it fails to recognize this fact and focus attention upon improvement at these stages."[46]

In each administrative agency there are generally two stages of adjudication. The first stage is informal, in which decisions are made on the basis of informal correspondence, conferences, interviews, and inspections, rather than on the basis of formal hearings. The second stage is formal, and becomes operative only when parties are dissatisfied with decisions made in the first stage, for all agencies attempt to settle cases informally. A possible exception to this rule exists where statutory provisions require that a hearing be given in a particular case category. The formal administrative process is, in the words of the Attorney General's Committee, marked by

> hearings in which testimony is taken, subject to cross-examination, and embodied into a record. . . . When formal hearings are held, the record is normally considered by officers of the agency and, after opportunity for oral argument before them, by the agency heads themselves. Thereafter the agency's final decision, except in comparatively few situations . . . is subject either by express statutory provision or by judicial construction, to complete judicial review on the law and more limited review on the facts.[47]

This is what might be termed the popular legal view of the formal stage of administrative adjudication; however, evidence will be presented at a later point to prove that only very rarely are the attributes considered essential actually present. In order to understand the informal administrative process it is necessary not only to investigate the initial stage of adjudication but also the extensive utilization of informal techniques within the *formal* stage itself.

Informal adjudicative methods were utilized in the administrative process from the very beginning. In its first annual report the ICC stated:

> The complaints made to the Commission [with regard to receiving damages from carriers] have been very numerous. . . . In no case has the Commission declined to give attention to a complaint because of its being informal or imperfectly presented, but when not in shape for its action, if the facts indicated a probable grievance, it has opened correspondence with the carrier with a view to redress. In the majority of cases the correspondence has resulted in satisfactory arrangement. Either the complainant has been found to be mistaken in his facts, or if wronged it has been through the carelessness or mistake of an agent which the carrier readily corrected, or if the facts presented a case of difference of opinion, the parties, when brought into communi-

cation, succeeded in finding some basis for settlement without further intervention. This method of disposing of complaints is believed by the Commission to be more useful than any other, because its tendency is towards the establishment of desirable relations between the carriers and those who must be their customers. . . .[48]

The ICC, destined to become the prototype of future agencies, found from the very beginning that legal formalities do not promote the disposition of cases. Formal adversary proceedings tend to promote discord between parties resulting in a needless increase in litigation.

In its annual report of 1901 the ICC distinguished between and commented upon the differences between formal and informal adjudication in the following manner:

> The work of the Commission which pertains directly to regulation involves two distinct kinds of procedure. One based upon formal petitions filed with the Commission . . . , and involving regular hearing and investigation, the preparation of a report setting forth the material facts found and conclusions reached by the Commission, and issuance of an order dismissing the case or directing the carrier or carriers complained against to correct the rate or practice which may be held unlawful. The other kind of procedure arises in the performance by the Commission of its duty, under the twelfth section, to "execute and enforce the provisions of the act," and relates to complaints presented by letter, the examination of tariffs on file in the office in connection with such complaints, and correspondence with shippers and carriers concerning the same. Complaints of the latter class are called informal complaints. . . .
>
> No order can be issued upon an informal complaint or inquiry. The main object of that method of procedure is the speedy disposition, through settlements, readjustments plainly required by the statute, or advice given by the Commission, of matters on which regulation is demanded, and thus to limit the number of contested cases upon the docket. It would be an injustice to complaining shippers and communities, amounting frequently to denial of relief, to compel the institution of a regular proceeding every time cause

of complaint is brought to the attention of the Commission; and the number of cases requiring the hearing of witnesses, oral or written argument, and formulated decision would probably be greater than the Commission could dispose of properly or without intolerable delays. The great mass of complaints are handled and disposed of by the Commission by preliminary investigation and correspondence or conference with carriers and shippers. The matters considered and acted upon in this way range from overcharges upon small shipments to rate relations affecting the interests of entire communities, and are of the same nature as those which find their way to the regular case docket of the Commission.[49]

The use of informal procedure for the purpose of adjudication was so extensively employed by the ICC in its early stages of development that it was able to conclude by 1907 that:

> A fair conception of the work performed by the Commission in the field of regulation is not possible without reference to the results attained in respect to . . . cases in which formal complaint is not filed, nor proceedings of a formal nature pursued by the complainant. The public is not advised of the full extent of the work accomplished in securing, through correspondence, the voluntary adjustment by carriers of questions in dispute relating to interstate transportation, nor is the public cognizant of the extreme importance and value of the results attained.
>
> Through the medium of correspondence is secured the settlement of many matters extremely vexatious to shippers. . . . Controversies arising out of the relations between the carriers themselves are likewise, in many instances, presented to the Commission for arbitration. The Commission is also called upon frequently by traffic officials of carriers to indicate what is considered to be the proper and lawful course to be pursued in respect to the applications of rates or regulations affecting transportation.[50]

The second important area involving the extensive utilization of informal procedure is *within the formal hearing stage* itself. Contrary to the popular scholarly view, full-fledged legal procedure (notice, hearing with cross-examination, a record with adequate findings to support conclusions, and decisions based upon hearing records with the opportunity for court review) is rarely employed. Procedure in the formal stage is shortened through the use of prehearing conferences and conferences during the course of the proceedings. With regard to the trend to simplify the formal administrative process, the ICC again reflected this from the very beginning, as illustrated in its first annual report:

> It has been deemed exceedingly desirable that proceedings before the Commission on complaints against carriers should be made as informal as should be consistent with order and regularity, and that dilatory action of every nature should be discouraged. The rules of procedure made no other requirement for a complaint than that it should be in the form of a verified petition and set forth the facts which constitute the grievance complained of. When such a statement has appeared . . . the petition has been accepted and an answer called for. . . . The defendant has been expected to disclose its defense by answer, so that one hearing may be sufficient for the final disposition of the case.
>
> By this method of procedure technicalities are discarded, the complaints and the answers to them are treated as presenting business controversies which the parties, if they elect so to do, can manage for themselves (without legal aid). . . . When parties have managed their own cases the taking of testimony has been somewhat informal also, and the Commission has given its aid in the examination of witnesses produced, in order that the whole truth . . . might . . . be brought out and made plain. It is a pleasure to note that in this informal mode of procedure the parties have in general most heartily cooperated, and that they have been very liberal in agreeing upon the facts when it was practicable to do so, thereby materially shortening the hearings and making them assume more the form of amicable contentions.[51]

In summary, there is a trend in administrative law, perhaps indigenous to administrative adjudication, toward the development and utilization of informal procedure, characterized by correspondence, conference, and investigation rather than by procedure judicial in nature patterned upon the common law. No study has yet been made of the employment of informal procedure in the administrative process other than that contained in the monographs of the Attorney General's Committee on Administrative Procedure published in 1941. In terms of legal theory, a description and analysis of the use of informal procedure in administrative adjudication is important because it is a magnification of the general problem presented to legal theory by the development of administrative law. At the first line of defense, common-law theory demands that adjudication be handled by the courts; however, because this is evidently impossible in the modern administrative state, common-law theory demands the formalization of the administrative process in accordance with legal standards, with the opportunity for judicial review. Informal administrative adjudication, on the other hand, cannot be subjected to common-law forms by definition, nor are decisions made in this manner subject to judicial review, because of the legal doctrine of exhaustion of administrative remedy and more practical difficulties involved in taking a case to court. To the extent that informal procedure pervades the administrative process, a serious antithesis to the common law is present. An analysis of the quantitative and qualitative significance of informal procedure in the administrative process constitutes the remaining sections of this book.

Chapter II

SHORTENED PROCEDURE IN THE FORMAL ADMINISTRATIVE PROCESS

An examination of the formal administrative process would normally involve an analysis of formal hearings and provisions for judicial review; however, a significant movement has taken place in American administrative law to shorten or eliminate altogether formal hearings required by statute or regulation through the utilization of informal negotiation. Formal hearings may be required by statute or regulation, or the parties themselves may request hearing, either because informal settlement has failed or because they feel that the case will be more fairly adjudicated through the process of formal hearing. In any analysis of the limitations that administrative agencies have placed upon the formal hearing process it is important to understand the essential legal position of the right to a hearing. Moreover, the development of the concept of shortened procedure in theory is necessary, and certain pertinent examples of the use of shortened procedure will be noted here. Finally, an assessment of the significance of this procedure will conclude the preceding remarks.

OPPORTUNITY TO BE HEARD

In the last chapter it was noted that due process of law in administrative proceedings requires, ideally, an adequate hearing in most cases of adjudication. The nature of the legal requirement varies, however, in accordance with statutory and constitutional criteria. These, in turn, usually depend upon the nature of the administrative function at issue and the significance of the action being taken. Bernard Schwartz has pointed out that "the applicability of the notice and hearing requirements of procedural due process . . . is largely based upon the distinction between the legislative or rule-making functions of administrative agencies, on the one hand, and their judicial or adjudicative activities, on the other. In rule-making, there is usually no right to

31

be heard in the absence of statutory provisions therefor. . . . Insofar as adjudicatory functions are concerned, conformity with the basic judicial standards of notice and hearing is normally held to be essential." [1] This, at least, is an ideal of the judiciary. In fact there are numerous cases of adjudication where judicial standards are not applicable in the formal administrative stage, and they are never applicable in the informal stage.[2]

To illustrate this general judicial concept, consider *Bi-Metallic Co.* v. *Colorado* (1915),[3] in which the Court upheld an order of the State Board of Equalization of Colorado, increasing the valuation of all taxable property in Denver by 40 per cent. The plaintiff contended that: "There was no hearing; there was no notice; the rights of the property owner were ignored, and the decision of the Supreme Court of the State sustaining the order of the boards was state action depriving the taxpayer of property without due process of law, in violation of the provisions of the Fourteenth Amendment." [4] Speaking for the majority of the Court, which upheld the state action, Holmes said:

> Where a rule of conduct applies to more than a few people it is unpracticable that everyone should have a direct voice in its adoption. The Constitution does not require all public acts to be done in town meeting or an assembly of the whole. General statutes within the state power are passed that affect the person or property of individuals, sometimes to the point of ruin, without giving them a chance to be heard. Their rights are protected in the only way that they can be in a complex society, by their power, immediate or remote, over those who make the rule. . . . There must be a limit to individual argument in such matters if government is to go on.[5]

Because of the size of the group affected by administrative action in the *Bi-Metallic* case a hearing was not necessary.

In *Londoner* v. *Denver* (1908),[6] a relatively small group of landowners was affected by a tax assessment of a local board for paving a street touching their property. Because such action bordered on adjudication, the Court held that the taxpayer must have an opportunity to be heard.

Further, with regard to rules of general application, Brandeis' opinion in the *Assigned Car Cases* (1927)[7] stated that "in establishing a rule of general application, it is not a condition of its validity that there be adduced evidence of its appropriateness in respect to every railroad to which it will be applicable. In this connection, the Commission, like other legislators, may reason from the particular to the general." [8]

Rate-making, usually considered legislative, frequently has specific applicability making it in such instances an adjudicative function.[9] In specific rate-making proceedings the courts have held that due process requires notice and hearing.[10] A possible contradiction to this decisional trend is evident in *Bowles* v. *Willingham* (1944);[11] however, the decision was made during time of war, so that the case must be considered abnormal.

With regard to the general adjudicative activities of administrative agencies, statutes delegating judicial power usually provide for notice and hearing. Exceptions, however, do exist.[12] The significance of such administrative hearings is limited in cases requiring immediate action in which the courts have upheld the administrative practice of eliminating hearings prior to taking action.[13] For example, one cannot obtain a formal hearing to establish the legality of the collection of internal revenue.[14] In general, in such emergency cases judicial review is relied upon to give the individual protection from arbitrary administrative action.

The distinction between opportunity for hearing in adjudicative proceedings, on the one hand, and rule-making proceedings on the other, was maintained by the Administrative Procedure Act of 1946.[15] Where rule-making is involved the requirements of section 4 apply, and this essentially means that only the required notice of proposed rule-making must be given. Further, section 4 includes several broad escape clauses which further limit formal procedure. Even though formal procedure in rule making may not be required by statute, and hence not by the Administrative Procedure Act,[16] in some cases such procedure can be required, if rules have particular applicability making the decision essentially adjudicative.[17] Under certain circumstances due process can require hearing even if there is no statutory provision for hearing.[18]

With regard to formal rule-making, where the statute requires that rules be made on the record after the agency affords opportunity for a hearing, sections 7 and 8 of the Administrative Procedure Act apply. It is important to note that section 7(c) of the APA provides: "In rule-making or determining claims for money or benefits or applications for initial licenses any agency may, where the interest of any party will not be prejudiced thereby, adopt procedures for the submission of all or part of the evidence in written form." On the other hand, the provisions of the APA are rigid in establishing formal procedure where formal adjudication is required by statute.

THE CONCEPT OF SHORTENED PROCEDURE IN THEORY

Although it is evident that in some cases an opportunity for a hearing must be offered by administrative agencies, a strong administrative emphasis upon simplifying hearings, in order to save time and expense for both the government and the private party concerned, has developed. To a considerable extent, formal administrative hearings are limited by prehearing conferences of an informal nature in which the parties involved, on the basis of consent, settle certain points of disagreement between them and determine the nature of the hearing that is to be held. Such prehearing conferences are patterned on a court practice based upon Rule 16 of the Federal Rules of Civil Procedure, which provides that:

> In any action, the court may in its discretion direct the attorneys for the party to appear before it for a conference to consider
> (1) The simplification of the issues;
> (2) The necessity or desirability of amendments to the pleadings;
> (3) The possibility of obtaining admissions of fact and of documents which will avoid unnecessary proof;
> (4) The limitation of the number of expert witnesses;
> (5) The advisability of a preliminary reference of issues to a master for findings to be used as evidence when the trial is to be by jury;
> (6) Such other matters as may aid in the disposition of the action.[19]

Rule 16 further provides that the court should make an order, resulting from the conference, which would control subsequent formal proceedings.

The President's Conference on Administrative Procedure—1953

The Report of the President's Conference on Administrative Procedure, issued in 1953, strongly recommended administrative utilization of prehearing conferences to resolve issues. In this regard, the Conference report recommended that all agencies "require that in all proceedings the issues to be adjudicated be made initially as precise as possible, in order that hearing officers may proceed promptly to conduct the hearings on relevant and material matter only. . . ." [20] Further, the Conference report felt that all agencies should "encourage hearing officers to call and conduct prehearing conferences and *other conferences during hearings,* with a view to the simplification, clarification, and disposition of the issues involved, and with a further view to the shortening of the proof on the issues." [21] Finally, in attempting to adapt Rule 16, utilized by the courts, to administrative adjudication, the President's Conference recommended that all agencies adopt the following rule, or one similar to it:

> In any proceeding the agency or its designated hearing officer upon its or his own motion, or upon the motion of one of the parties . . . , may in its or his discretion direct the parties or their qualified representatives to appear at a specified time and place for a conference to consider
> (a) the simplification of the issues;
> (b) the necessity of amendments to the pleadings;
> (c) the possibility of obtaining stipulations, admissions of facts and of documents;
> (d) the limitation of the number of expert witnesses;
> (e) such other matters as may aid in the disposition of the proceeding.
> The agency or its designated hearing officer shall make an order which recites the action taken at the conference . . . , and which limits the issues for hearing to those not disposed of by admissions or agreements; and such order shall control the subsequent course of the proceeding unless modified for good cause by subsequent order." [22]

It is evident that this rule is directly patterned upon Rule 16, with perhaps greater emphasis placed upon the necessity for such prehearing conferences for the purpose of controlling formal proceedings.

In commenting upon the use of prehearing conferences by administrative agencies the Conference report stated:

> Agencies' rules vary widely on the matter of pre-hearing conferences. In some agencies such conferences are mandatory in certain cases. In other agencies, in the absence of request of the parties, conferences apparently can only be called on motion of the agency. In still others, they apparently can be called only at the request of the parties. . . . All agencies, by rule or otherwise, should urge hearing officers to encourage, at every opportunity, round-table meetings of the parties prior to the commencement of hearings, with the view of culling out those issues upon which there is no real controversy, crystallizing, sorting, simplifying, and analyzing the others. . . .

> It is believed that prehearing conferences could be profitably held in most cases. Frank and informal discussion many times dissipates a reticence and reluctance to agree which exist for no good reason other than the absence of a qualified, disinterested mediator. . . .

> Another significant value to be gained by holding prehearing conferences is the formulation of a plan for the efficient conduct of the hearing. . . .

> In addition, a more generous use of conferences during the course of the hearing would aid in the further narrowing of issues and would stimulate stipulations and agreements between the parties, thereby further shortening records.[23]

In summary, the report of the President's Conference on Administrative Procedure reflects the general trend evident outside of and within the administrative branch to shorten formal adjudication as much as possible. This trend is characterized by the desire to replace the technicalities of formal proceedings with the flexibility of informal conferences. Those who support this trend question the efficacy of formal proceedings in relation to informal conferences, both with regard to securing efficient operation and with regard to obtaining justice.

Trial Examiner's View

The need for a vast improvement in pretrial methods is manifested in the views of J. D. Bond, who as a Federal Communications Commission hearing examiner, writing for the *Journal of the Federal Communications Bar Associaton,* noted the importance of "the achievement of smaller records in shorter and less expensive hearings, and thus the gain of quicker and more certain justice for those citizens who toil in the mazes of hearing proceedings. They have a right . . . to less tedious justice. Pretrial . . . is a remedial measure of tremendous potential, but largely unrealized, value." [24] Noting the tremendous growth of pretrial techniques in the federal and state courts, Bond feels that "the uncomfortable truth is that whereas the processes of the courts were being rapidly improved and expedited, the hearing processes of the agencies and departments of the Federal government generally remained virtually at a standstill. It has been said, and with a measure of justification, that the utility of the hearing process for deciding controversies more expeditiously than in the courts is too often all but lost in some modern-day proceedings. . . . Many present-day administrative hearing decisions could have been derived more expeditiously, more economically, and upon a much smaller record through pre-trial, trial and decision in a court of law." [25] Such a view is an indictment of the formal administrative process, and it is the prevalence of such views that has caused the present emphasis upon the necessity for infusing the formal administrative process with informal techniques.

THE USE OF SHORTENED PROCEDURE BY ADMINISTRATIVE AGENCIES:
THE ICC, CAB, AND SEC

The Interstate Commerce Commission provides an interesting case study in the area of the development of informal methods in the formal adjudicative stage. Shortened procedure was first developed by the Interstate Commerce Commission in 1923. The 1923 annual report of the ICC states:

> With a view to simplifying, shortening, and making less expensive the procedure upon complaints filed with us, we have been experimenting during the year with a new method

of handling the simpler *formal cases.* This shortened procedure consists of dispensing with the usual method of holding hearings before a commissioner or an examiner, and substituting sworn statements of fact.

After the respective memoranda have been filed, the case is assigned to an examiner, who studies them as he would a formal record, and who then prepares a proposed report. At any time up to the date when such report is issued, any party to the case may request the regular formal hearing either upon the whole complaint or upon certain features of it.

Oral argument may be had upon reasonable request therefor. . . .

A substantial number of attorneys and traffic officials practicing before us have stated that they believe our experiment is a step in the right direction and that many of our formal cases can doubtless, *with the consent of the parties,* be disposed of in the manner suggested.[26]

The original ICC shortened procedure provided for oral argument if requested, and, as now, depended upon the consent of the parties in order to be put into practice. In general, the worth of this form of shortened procedure depended upon the extent to which hearings could be entirely eliminated through the use of written memoranda for the purpose of establishing the facts of a particular case.

In commenting upon the use of shortened procedure by the ICC, the staff of the Attorney General's Committee on Administrative Procedure noted that shortened procedure is requested either by a private party or by the Commission; however "the shortened procedure is suggested to the parties in approximately twice as many cases as the number in which the parties consent."[27] From the very beginning, the necessity of obtaining the consent of the parties to effect shortened procedure was an obstacle to its effectiveness.[28]

When the ICC used shortened procedure the primary facts of the case under consideration were not in dispute; therefore the need for a formal hearing, with cross-examination and so on, was nonexistent. A former chief of the Shortened Procedure Section of the ICC estimated that the facts were contradicted in the memoranda of the parties in only one case out of twenty.[29] Further, with regard to the efficacy of this method of resolving disputes, some members of the staff of the Attorney General's Committee on Administrative Procedure were "firmly of the opinion that the shortened procedure sometimes results in better decisions than hearing procedures, by reason of the greater precision that is possible when facts are stated in writing rather than orally." [30] Before the Second World War, approximately 33 per cent of all formal cases were settled through shortened procedure each year.

Because of the need for obtaining the consent of the parties to a dispute before using shortened procedure, it was felt by the Commission that the use of informal techniques in the formal administrative process was unnecessarily burdened. Not only did the ICC shortened procedure, as it developed, require the consent of the parties; there was no provision for a modified hearing, and if oral argument was desired the entire case under consideration had to be shifted into the formal hearing stage.

To overcome these obstacles to the effective limitation of the formal hearing process, in 1942 the ICC adopted what was termed a *modified* procedure, which differed from shortened procedure in that the consent of the parties did not have to be obtained, and oral argument was permitted in certain cases without necessitating the shifting of the case into the formal process.

The Rules of Practice of the ICC provide that if modified procedure is to be used, either by order of the Commission[31] or by desire of the parties, statements of fact with regard to a particular case, together with exhibits, are to be filed in writing by the defendant, followed by the rebuttal of the complainant.[32] Further, "if cross examination of any witness is desired the name of the witness and the subject matter of the desired cross examination shall, together with any other request for oral hearing, including the basis therefor, be stated. . . ." [33] And "the order setting the proceeding for oral hearing, if hearing is deemed necessary, will specify the matters upon which the parties are not in agreement and respecting which oral evidence is to be introduced." [34] In this manner, under modified procedure, the ICC has adopted a selective formal procedure with regard to witnesses and evidence.

The extensive use of modified procedure began in 1952, and it was preceded by a change of thinking on the part of the ICC respecting shortened procedure. In the words of Commissioner Mahaffie:

> That change was a belief that unnecessary time and effort was being expended in obtaining consent of the parties to use of shortened procedure, and that procedural improvements could be made. Accordingly, respecting Bureau of Formal Cases proceedings, it was concluded experimentally to switch to modified procedure. . . .
>
> The results of increased use of modified procedure have been very gratifying. The elapsed time in disposing of such proceedings has been reduced, and substantial monetary savings to both the Commission and the parties also have resulted. . . . Investigation - and - suspension   proceedings (very infrequently handled under shortened procedure) lend themselves very well to modified procedure handling. . . . Another development during the period in question has been increased use of modified procedure in certain proceedings in the Section of Complaints of the Bureau of Motor Carriers. Contemporaneously, use of shortened procedure has declined, and as of April 30, 1954, only six such proceedings were pending on the Commission's entire docket.[35]

Modified procedure has replaced shortened procedure in the operation of the ICC. The increase in the number of cases settled by modified procedure indicates its greater flexibility and usefulness. Further, this procedure has been employed in effecting settlement of complex cases, whereas shortened procedure, in general, could not be utilized in this manner.

Oral hearing has rarely been requested under modified procedure. Between October, 1952, and April, 1954 (inclusive), there were only 6 requests for cross-examination or other oral hearing, out of 1,130 modified procedure cases.[36] Former Commissioner Mahaffie of the ICC noted that even where requests for oral hearing were made, "the resulting hearing, being restricted to cross-examination, or other limited purpose, has taken but a fraction of the time that otherwise would have been necessary had the proceeding been orally conducted throughout." [37]

In these modified procedure cases where the ICC is able to bring about settlement without oral argument (over 99 per cent of the cases), it is, in essence, settling cases by obtaining the informal consent of the parties. Therefore, although the procedure is formal in name, it is informal in substance.

The significance of the use of modified procedure in the formal administrative process of the ICC can be observed in the accompanying table.

ICC—PER CENT OF FORMAL RATE PROCEEDINGS HANDLED
BY MODIFIED PROCEDURE

Kind of rate proceeding	Fiscal year			
	1958	1959	1960	1961
	(%)	(%)	(%)	(%)
Other than motor carrier:				
Formal complaints	51	73	37	69
Investigation and suspension	35	19	31	49
Motor carriers:				
Formal complaints	32	71	45	38
Investigation and suspension	88	75	42	87
Other rate proceedings:*				
Motor				59
Rail				20

SOURCE: 1961 ICC Annual Report, p. 46.
* These proceedings include investigations without suspension, section 4, section 5a, and released rates applications as well as ex parte proceedings. Figures were unavailable in these categories prior to 1961.

Certain arguments have been advanced in opposition to this extensive use of modified procedure from various lawyers dealing with the ICC. It has been stated that the lack of a full oral hearing prevents the examiner from understanding in full all of the facets of a particular case; information developed from written memoranda is not entirely adequate in this regard. Further, demeanor evidence is of importance but of course requires oral hearing. Again, it has been stated that lack of oral hearing encourages "claim sharks" [38] to file complaints with the ICC which would not stand the test of a full hearing, both because of inadequate evidence and because complainants cannot bother to appear in formal hearing, the complaint not justifying the expense involved. Finally, it has been argued against modified procedure that time is really not saved by avoiding oral hearing; even under modified procedure it takes approximately 300 days between filing and decision.[39]

In summary, the Interstate Commerce Commission has adopted a form of modified procedure which eliminates the need for hearings in the formal administrative process. The Commission has used the practice of ordering the parties to a dispute to submit their controversy to settlement through the use of this procedure, and thereby it has greatly increased the effectiveness of modified procedure in relation to shortened procedure, for the latter practice required the Commission to obtain the consent of the parties before eliminating a formal hearing. Although the parties have the opportunity to present segments of their dispute for settlement based upon an oral hearing under modified procedure, they do so in less than 1 per cent of the cases settled in this way. The success of this procedure, evident from an examination of the percentage of cases settled by this practice, suggests that those subject to the jurisdiction of the ICC are satisfied with its use; although certain traditional criticisms have been leveled at the limitation of formal hearings by modified procedure, such criticisms do not seem to be widespread. Finally, it should be noted that the use of modified procedure by the ICC goes far beyond the concept of prehearing conferences in theory and in practice. In general, modified procedure eliminates hearings, whereas prehearing conferences define the scope of the hearing. The use of prehearing conferences by the ICC will be discussed at a later point, in conjunction with the practices of other agencies in this field.

The Civil Aeronautics Board

A further significant case study in the area of shortened procedure in the formal administrative process is presented by certain phases of the operation of the Civil Aeronautics Board. The Civil Aeronautics Act requires hearings with respect to application cases, where application is made for certificates of public convenience and necessity and for foreign air carrier permits.[40] Further, in airmail rate proceedings orders are to be made only after notice and hearings.[41] These provisions were not changed by the Federal Aviation Act of 1958. It is interesting to observe that the staff of the Attorney General's Committee on Administrative Procedure felt that the hearing requirement with respect to certificates and permits was unwise. With regard to the provisions relating to airmail rate proceedings the Attorney General's staff noted: "True, the statute says that orders are to be made after notice and hearing. Elsewhere in the administration of the act, however, like requirements have been interpreted as connoting only that notice be given and that a hearing be held if desired by the parties. . . . The whole subsidy program, it is believed, could be carried forward more expeditiously and without the paraphernalia of examiners' reports, exceptions, briefs, and the like if it were subjected to a process of negotiation and consultation, rather than directed toward the holding of formal hearings." [42] In this area, regardless of statutory provisions to the contrary, the staff of the Attorney General's Committee felt that in the settlement of airmail rate cases formal proceedings were not as effective as informal negotiation and consultation.

In the light of the remarks of the Attorney General's Committee staff it is interesting to observe that in 1942 the CAB adopted a new shortened procedure with regard to compensation to carriers for the transportation of airmail. In its annual report of that year the Board stated:

> The major objective sought by the Board in prescribing a new procedure was to accord the carrier and any other interested party an opportunity for a full hearing, while at the same time expediting final disposition of the case. The show-cause procedure adopted by the Board achieves this end by placing before the carrier a complete statement of a proposed disposition of the rate proceeding by the Board, and then affording the carrier an opportunity to contest any such portions of that statement as do not meet with its agreement. By this method all interested persons are fully informed of the Board's tentative conclusions. To the extent that the parties are in agreement . . . there is no occasion for further procedure of any kind. Accordingly, the issues in any hearing in a rate case are effectively limited to those

concerning which there is a real controversy. It is no longer necessary for the carrier or other persons to introduce extensive testimony and lengthy argument on matters simply to guard against the possibility that the Board might dispose of them contrary to the parties' views.[43]

In this manner the Board, rather than automatically granting a hearing, merely gave the parties subject to the decision of the CAB in a particular airmail rate case an *opportunity* for a hearing.

A further limitation of formal procedure in the airmail rate field has been the adoption by the CAB of an informal conference procedure *before a show-cause order is issued.* In 1948 the Board noted that:

> Because of the transitional nature of the periods through which the carriers were passing, the difficulties were greatly increased in establishing final rates for the future, as well as for the substantial periods that have accumulated with the filing of petitions. If rates were to be established within a reasonable time, a way had to be found to shorten the normal procedures. It was felt that considerable time and effort could be saved in the long run if, in advance of the issuance of a show-cause order, the Board's staff and the carrier met for the purpose of developing all the facts essential to the establishment of a rate, as well as exchanging views toward a more thorough mutual understanding of the carriers' problems. In that way, it was hoped that many issues would be resolved in accordance with well-established principles, and those issues that remained would be clearly defined. Thus the time that normally elapses between the issuance of a show-cause order and the final establishment of a rate would be considerably shortened. Accordingly, the Board officially authorized certain conference procedures on November 14, 1947.[44]

It should be noted here that the CAB has not only attempted to supplant formal airmail rate hearings with informal conferences for the purpose of expediting business, but has also developed informal procedure to establish a more effective modus vivendi with the groups coming under its jurisdiction. Formal procedure and adversary hearings do not establish the type of mutual understanding that is necessary for effective regulation.

Because of the success of these informal conferences before the issuance of show-cause orders, the present Rules of Practice of the CAB set forth the procedure in detail. With regard to the invocation of informal airmail rate conference procedure, the rule is that "conferences between members of the Board's staff, representatives of air carriers, the Post Office Department and other interested persons may be called by the Board's staff for the purpose of considering and clarifying issues and factual material in pending proceedings for the establishment of rates for the transportation of mail." [45]

Further, with regard to the scope of the conferences, it is specified that "the mail rate conferences shall be limited to the discussion of, and possible agreement on, particular issues and related factual material in accordance with sound rate-making principles." [46] Recommendations are to be made to the Board on the basis of these conferences.

Information obtained from these informal conferences is to remain secret until the Board makes a decision, or until 90 days have elapsed after the termination of the conference.[47] Data requested by the Board which is defined in general by the Rules of Practice,[48] must be submitted by the carrier concerned. Then "after a careful analysis of these data, the Board's staff will, in most cases, send the carrier what might be termed a statement of exceptions showing areas of differences. Where practicable, the carrier may submit its answer to these exceptions. Conferences will then be scheduled to work out a clear understanding and resolution of the issues and facts from the standpoint of sound rate-making principles." [49] Further, "the rate conferences not being in the nature of proceedings, no briefs, or argument, or any formal steps, will be entertained by the Board. The form, content and time of the staff's presentation to the Board are entirely matters of internal procedure. . . ." [50]

With regard to the legal effect of these informal conferences:

> No agreements or understanding reached in rate conferences as to facts or issues shall in any respect be binding on the Board or any participant. Any party to mail rate pro-

ceedings will have the same rights to file an answer and take other procedural steps as though no rate conference had been held. The fact, however, that rate conferences were held and certain agreements or understandings may have been reached on certain facts and issues renders it proper to provide that upon the filing of an answer by any party to the rate proceeding all issues going to the establishment of a rate shall be open, except insofar as limited in prehearing conference. . . .[51]

Although these conferences may have no binding legal effect, as is true in the case of prehearing conferences, in substance their effect does settle the case under consideration, except where irrevocable differences exist among the parties.

In 1952 the CAB, in a discussion of the trend to eliminate formal hearings with special reference to airmail rate proceedings, noted that new rules which incorporated the Board's practice in this area were "designed to expedite formal hearings, insure more uniform application of the rules, and to save time for the Board members, staff, and parties appearing before the Board by simplification of procedures." [52] Specifically, in the new Rules of Practice "the procedure providing for pro forma mail-rate hearings was eliminated, and written statements and informal negotiations are now utilized in lieu of formal hearings in certain commercial rate cases." [53]

Significantly, informal conferences are used by the CAB not only to simplify issues before formal orders are made governing the airmail rate field, but also to resolve disputed points during the course of formal hearings in this area. For example, in 1954 the Board noted that "by an increased use of informal conferences during the course of litigated mail-rate proceedings to resolve disputes such proceedings have been expedited." [54]

The Securities and Exchange Commission

The operations of the Securities and Exchange Commission present a final example outside the prehearing area of the administrative trend to limit the formal hearing process. The Securities Act of 1933, the Securities Exchange Act of 1934, and the Public Utility Holding Company Act of 1935 require formal hearings in certain cases.[55] The provisions of the Holding Company Act of

1935 generally require no more than an opportunity for hearing with respect to certain applications to and orders of the Commission. The staff of the Attorney General's Committee noted that "where the Commission itself is of the opinion that the application should be granted, and no person objects or requests a hearing, at least as far as the express statutory terminology is concerned, there appears to be no bar to dispensing with a hearing." [56] They also felt in this respect that "where the application or declaration presents no difficult problems and has no far-reaching consequences, dispensing with a, hearing is desirable. The Holding Company Act provides for extraordinarily close supervision over utilities; myriad minor transactions are required to be licensed by the Commission. The Commission and its staff even now devote an enormous amount of time to matters under the Holding Company Act; on the other hand, the utilities themselves are placed under considerable burden of time and expense if they are required to go to hearing in all cases." [57] The staff noted the "rarity with which persons appear and object at hearings on applications and declarations." [58]

The SEC took steps during the 'thirties to eliminate hearings where no substantial objection to a particular application or Commission order was present. For example, "the frequency with which respondents failed to appear in proceedings to suspend offering sheets of oil and gas interests ultimately led the Commission to adopt a rule under which a permanent order will be issued forthwith unless the person filing the offering sheet makes written requests for a hearing." [59] Further, with regard to Commission revocation of security registration for exchange trading, a rule was put into effect that if 40 days elapsed after a deficiency notice[60] was sent, and neither the issuer nor the exchange made a written request for a hearing, the registration was withdrawn automatically.[61] Again, with regard to applications by national securities exchanges for the extension of unlisted trading privileges to securities listed and registered on another national securities exchange, the SEC, in 1947, "put into effect a simplified procedure to eliminate hearings on applications for unlisted trading privileges in cases where none of the interested parties or public investors desire a hearing." [62] If there is no request for a hearing, the disposition of the application is based upon Commission files. This procedure was extended to applications for delisting of securities from exchange trading. Such procedure was further extended by the Commission into other areas in 1947.[63]

Aside from the elimination of hearings entirely, where no request is made for a hearing, the SEC limits the formal hearing process by an extensive use of informal conferences during the course of a formal proceeding. The Attorney General's staff noted that informal conferences "continue informally in the course of the hearing; it is not uncommon for counsel for the Commission and other counsel to call a recess during a hearing, confer over the method of procedure, and return shortly with an agreement on the best method of producing evidence or otherwise presenting the issues with a minimum of waste motion and maximum of expedition." [64] The present SEC procedural rules provide that "during the course of the hearing, the staff is generally available for informal discussions to reconcile bona fide divergent views not only between itself and other persons interested in the proceedings, but among all interested persons; and, when circumstances permit, the staff endeavors to narrow, if possible, the issues to be considered at the formal hearing." [65] This use of informal conferences during the course of formal proceedings was noted above with regard to the Civil Aeronautics Board. Such instances of the use of informal procedure demonstrate an administrative tendency to utilize informal procedures during the course of formal hearings if informal methods fail in settling the case before the formal hearing stage is reached.

THE USE OF PREHEARING CONFERENCES

Unquestionably one of the most widely used methods for the purpose of limitation and simplification of formal hearings throughout the administrative process is the prehearing conference. Modeled on a practice prevalent in the federal and state court systems, the prehearing conference is essentially an informal conference in which the agency and the parties involved participate for the purpose of limiting the scope of the hearing, thereby expediting the proceeding.

The Interstate Commerce Commission

In 1954 Commissioner Mahaffie of the Interstate Commerce Commission stated that:

> Contemporaneously with the increased use of modified procedure another related procedural experiment has been under way. But first the reason for it. All parties who have had experience in rate cases know that many pages of transcript are not helpful; and they cost money. At a hearing frequently large numbers of exhibits are literally thrown into the record without opportunity for previous study and with the necessary consequence of requests for continuance in the hearing. Lengthy testimony of a complex character is not easy to comprehend in the hearing room, nor can satisfactory cross-examination follow immediately upon its conclusion. Hence, cross-examination of witnesses may frequently be wasteful and not always conducive to a better understanding of the issues. . . . The opportunity to study carefully thought out and supported issues in advance of the hearing . . . tends to reduce materially the size of records and to facilitate orderly presentation and full understanding on the part of all concerned.[66]

Because of this problem the ICC began to employ its established prehearing procedure extensively in an attempt to limit subsequent oral hearing.

The rules of Practice of the ICC specify that parties to a proceeding may be directed, by the Commission or an officer thereof, to appear for a conference either prior to or during the course of a hearing.[67] Suggestions in writing may be requested for the purpose of expediting the proceedings. Conferences of this type are directed to consider: "(1) The simplification of issues; (2) The necessity or desirability of amending the pleadings either for the purpose of clarification, amplification, or limitation; (3) The possibility of making admissions of certain averments of fact or stipulations concerning the use by either or both parties of matters of public record, such as annual reports . . . , to the end of avoiding the unnecessary introduction of proof; (4) The procedure at the hearing; (5) The limitation of the

number of witnesses; (6) The propriety of prior mutual exchange between or among the parties of prepared testimony and
exhibits; and (7) Such other matters as may aid in the simplification of the evidence and disposition of the proceeding." [68] An
order, a stipulation, or a statement of agreement on the record
shall record and effect the results of the pretrial conference.[69]
The parties shall have an opportunity to present objections to
the record of the conference, but the final order, stipulation, or
agreement shall control the subsequent course of the proceeding
"unless modified to prevent manifest injustice." [70]

It is evident that this form of prehearing conference used by
the ICC is somewhat more extensive than that recommended for
use by the President's Conference on Administrative Procedure.[71]
To the extent to which these conferences are successful the subsequent formal hearing is deprived of any meaning. However, in
commenting upon pretrial procedure used by the ICC, a practitioner before that agency noted that:

> The opinion seems to be almost unanimous that pretrial
> conferences, while good in theory, have not worked very well
> in practice. In the first place, it is difficult to hold such con-
> ferences elsewhere than in Washington, which means that a
> great deal of expense is involved in traveling to and from
> the pretrial conference. I am inclined to agree . . . that
> while such conferences are helpful in court proceedings,
> they have not proved helpful in ICC practice. John Turney
> thinks that the pretrial conference has been too much of a
> "free-for-all town meeting" and that the "pretrial conference"
> is generally a farce. But Mr. Turney seems to believe that
> the pretrial conference could be made to work if the com-
> missioners and examiners would take them more seriously
> and work hard to bring about a clear definition of the issues
> and limitation of the scope of the proceeding before the
> hearing starts.[72]

Although the view among ICC practitioners seems to be skep-
tical, with respect to the value of prehearing conferences, a
genuine need for improving upon this procedure is recognized
by the Commission as well as by the practitioners.

The Securities and Exchange Commission

The procedural statement under which the Securities and Exchange Commission operates provides that "the hearing officer on his own motion may, or at the request of any party shall, call a conference of the parties at the opening of the hearing or at any subsequent time for the purpose of specifying and agreeing on the procedural steps to be followed or omitted in the proceeding." [73] Any such agreement with regard to procedure shall determine the course of the proceeding unless the parties themselves or the Commission, after notice, decide that a change is necessary. The use of prehearing conferences by the SEC dates to the 'thirties, and the staff of the Attorney General's Committee noted that "the Commission makes extensive use of the prehearing conference technique, especially in reference to cases issuing under the Holding Company Act." [74] The nature of these conferences has been described as follows by a former Chairman of the SEC: "We and our staff, before a hearing, try to assist the companies and their lawyers, accountants and engineers, so that the facts presented will lead to decisions which are both in accordance with the statute and business-like. In those preliminary discussions, we employ the informal method of the round-table conference. . . . We and those with whom we confer think out loud and in the vernacular; we and they put our feet on the table and unbutton our vests." [75] The success of these conferences is so great that normally "no substantial factual issues remain for the hearing, and, indeed, not seldom the only remaining purpose of the hearing is to make a record which will embody and support the fruits of the conferences. It seems clear that the Commission has been highly successful in simplifying and diminishing the usual formal litigious process through its conference technique." [76]

Because of the complexity of the operations of the SEC, prehearing conferences are used to "assist" the parties, not only in agreeing among themselves but to arrive at businesslike decisions. To a considerable extent these conferences have in essence replaced the formal hearing. In this way, even though a hearing may be required by law, effective prehearing conferences can reduce such hearings to mere formalities.

The Civil Aeronautics Board

The Civil Aeronautics Board provides for prehearing conferences where formal procedure is deemed necessary and where hearings are required by law. The CAB Rules of Practice state that:

> Prior to any hearings there will ordinarily be a prehearing conference before an Examiner. . . . Written notice of the prehearing conference shall be sent by the Chief Examiner to all parties to a proceeding and to other persons who appear to have an interest in such proceeding. The purpose of such a conference is to define and simplify the issues and the scope of the proceeding, to secure statements of the positions of the parties, . . . to schedule the exchange of exhibits before the date set for hearing, and to arrive at such agreements as will aid in the conduct and disposition of the proceeding. For example, consideration will be given to: (1) Matters which the Board can consider without the necessity of proof; (2) admissions of fact and the genuineness of documents; (3) admissibility of evidence; (4) limitation of the number of witnesses; (5) reducing of oral testimony to exhibit form; (6) procedure at the hearing, etc. If necessary, the Examiner may require further conference, or responsive pleadings, or both. The Examiner may also on his own motion or on motion of any party direct any party to a proceeding (air carrier or non-air carrier) to prepare and submit exhibits setting forth studies . . . relevant to the issues in the proceeding.[77]

This form of prehearing conference is similar to that employed by other administrative agencies under examination.

After the prehearing conference, "the Examiner shall issue a report of the prehearing conference, defining the issues, giving an account of the results of the conference, specifying a schedule for the exchange of exhibits and rebuttal exhibits. . . ."[78] This prehearing report is then sent to the parties to the proceeding. These parties may file objections to the report, and on the basis of these objections the examiner may issue a new report. The final report "shall constitute the official account of the conference and shall control the subsequent course of the proceeding, but it may be reconsidered and modified at any time to protect the public interest or to prevent injustice." [79]

Further, under the CAB Rules of Practice, the examiners have a general power to "hold conferences, before or during the hearing, for the settlement or simplification of issues." [80] These conferences are supplementary to the regular prehearing conferences.

The CAB prehearing conference procedure is an old one. The staff of the Attorney General's Committee noted that "the prehearing conference procedure was first employed in proceedings for the fixing of airmail rates, where its success caused it to be extended . . . to proceedings on new route applications. The result has been to shorten hearings and to reduce the cost of transcribing the record of the hearing." [81] In 1941 the CAB stated that prehearing conferences "are held in the great majority of economic cases, and experience has shown that they aid materially in expediting the procedure and in avoiding delays resulting from the introduction of new exhibits at the last minute which catch opposing counsel by surprise." [82]

An example of a prehearing conference case is the following:

> The applicant seeks to operate along the routes of several major air carriers a supplemental service which would pick up mail at many small towns at which the larger planes could stop neither profitably nor physically. The air carriers have no objection to the establishment of the proposed service if they can be assured that the applicant will not eventually establish a competing nonstop service. The prehearing conference was devoted largely to an exploration of the possibilities of providing such assurance as an alternative to intervention by the existing air carriers in the proceeding. This case suggests the potential advantages to be obtained by an informal show of cards. [83]

In this instance an informal conference averted an adversary hearing, to the advantage of all concerned.

The Federal Communications Commission

The Federal Communications Commission exhibits the same trend to limit the formal hearing process through prehearing conferences as those agencies that have already been examined. The Rules of Practice provided for the calling of a prehearing conference at the initiation of the Commission or an officer thereof, or at the request of any party to the proceeding. Further, an informal conference may be called during the course of a hearing.[84] Such conferences are directed to consider among other things: "(1) The necessity or desirability of simplification, clarification, amplification, or limitation of the issues; (2) The possibility of stipulating with respect to the facts; (3) The procedure at the hearing; (4) The limitation of the number of witnesses; (5) In cases arising under Title II of the Communications Act, the necessity or desirability of amending the pleadings and offers of settlement or proposals of adjustment." [85] The results of the conference, including any agreements reached between the parties themselves, will be incorporated (subject to the approval of the Hearing Examiner) into an order controlling subsequent proceedings.[86]

With regard to the limitation of the formal hearing process the FCC noted in 1954:

> One of the current major objectives of the Commission is to reduce the hearing procedure to bare essentials. One step has been to open hearings with a conference in which the parties can agree on fundamental facts which need not be gone into in the subsequent argument. This antedates but reflects the Government's interest in simplifying the hearing process through the President's Conference on Administrative Procedure. . . .
>
> In addition, the Commission, where possible to do so, makes findings on basic qualifications of competing applicants (legal, financial, and technical) before designating them for hearing. This has helped to eliminate testimony upon which no controversy exists.
>
> The Commission and the bar are working together to reduce the amount of oral testimony at hearings, and to make the hearing record a written one insofar as possible. . . . As of February 17, 1954, the Commission limited the number of pleadings that may be filed in these proceedings. This was done because numerous and repetitious pleadings have delayed and complicated consideration of cases. . . . The

Commission also believes that briefer "briefs" would help to expedite the hearing procedure.[87]

It is evident from this statement that the Commission wants to reduce oral testimony to a minimum. Further, it has found that in determining the legal, financial, and technical qualifications of applicants the hearing process is not always appropriate. Important adjudicative decisions are made in this area without benefit of hearing.

The development of prehearing techniques by the FCC stemmed from a necessity to increase the volume of adjudicative decisions. For a period before 1952, the FCC had maintained a "freeze" on the expansion of television stations, but in 1952 strong pressure was exerted upon it to expand the number of television stations and thereby increase coverage throughout the nation. This required the Commission to expedite application cases with regard to new and expanded television stations. A number of procedures were altered to meet the need for expediting applications, and among the more important changes was the rule providing for prehearing conferences. The Bar Association commented with respect to this rule: "Certainly the most constructive Commission achievement . . . was its adoption on February 6, 1953, of an amended Rule 1.841 [now 1.111] providing for a prehearing conference. . . . This pioneer step . . . resulted from the . . . desire 'to speed up the administrative process,' . . . by shortening and expediting the many hearings that stood in the way of the early initiation of television service."[88] It was noted, moreover, that "those hearings already held under revised Section 1.841 make clear that this new prehearing conference will sharpen and limit the issues in a hearing and result in the hoped-for savings of time and effort therein."[89]

The National Labor Relations Board and the Federal Trade Commission

As final examples, the operation of the National Labor Relations Board and the Federal Trade Commission both exhibit the use of informal conferences in the formal hearing process. The Rules of Practice of the NLRB state only that the trial examiners may "hold conferences for the settlement or simplification of the issues by consent of the parties, but not to adjust cases."[90] A further limitation to the formal process used by the NLRB stems from section 10(c) of the National Labor Relations Act which provides that unless the parties to a proceeding before the Board file exceptions to a proposed report and recommended order of an examiner, "such recommended order shall become the order of the Board and become effective as therein prescribed." [91] It has been noted with regard to this provision that "the finality which thus flows from the absence of exception is, in effect, the consequences of a consent determination. . . ." [92]

The Federal Trade Commission uses a prehearing procedure similar to the procedures that have already been discussed, whereby the hearing examiner may direct all the parties to a proceeding to meet with him to limit and define the scope and procedure of the formal hearing through simplifying the issues, limiting the number of witnesses, introducing stipulations of fact rather than using oral testimony, and the like.[93] From the very beginning, moreover, the FTC began to use stipulations of fact in formal proceedings. In 1918, the Commission stated:

> It has been the policy of the legal department . . . to bring, whenever possible, formal proceedings to a conclusion by stipulation or agreement as to the facts, thereby reducing the volume of litigation, resulting in a saving of time and expense. . . . This has been accomplished by submitting cases to the Commission for its consideration and determination upon agreed statements of facts wherein it is stipulated between the counsel for the Commission and the respondents, that the Commission shall proceed forthwith upon such agreed statements of facts to make and enter its findings and order to cease and desist from the practices charged without the introduction of evidence.[94]

This method has always been used by the Commission to limit oral testimony.

CONCLUSION

The administrative trend toward the limitation of the formal administrative process reflects a general administrative and legal approval of this development. In general, various forms of shortened procedure, which in fact eliminate the significance of the oral hearing, if not the hearing itself, are successful because the particular nature of many administrative determinations precludes the need for adversary hearings. As the staff of the Attorney General's Committee noted:

In the typical case tried in a court of law, there is frequently conflicting testimony by lay witnesses as to matters of ordinary fact; as a corollary, there is a distinct advantage in having the witnesses personally testify before the court in order that their veracity may be gauged from their conduct and demeanor. In a proceeding to fix rates or to determine the need for additional transportation facilities, much of the evidence is documentary in character, presented in the form of exhibits, and it is safe to say that at least 90 percent of the material which is presented by direct testimony of witnesses could as well have been prepared in exhibit form. The information relevant to the fixing of rates is largely taken from the records of the carrier and the [Board] . . . and relates to such matters as traffic trends and operating costs. Conflicts as to the accuracy of data involving a determination of the veracity of particular witnesses are almost nonexistent.[95]

Although the staff was in this instance speaking of the Civil Aeronautics Board, their conclusions could be extended to the other agencies under consideration because of the basic similarity of the procedural problems. It can be seen that the essential reason for the extensive development of various forms of shortened procedure in the administrative process is that both the government agencies and the parties under their jurisdiction have found that justice can be realized and time and expense saved through limitation of the formal administrative process. The facts with respect to a particular case can be developed either independently by the agency or through the introduction of various forms of exhibits and stipulations of fact. The trend will undoubtedly be toward greater limitation upon formal administrative procedures in the future.

Certain criticisms have been advanced against the widespread use of informal techniques in the formal stage of the administrative process. Representatives of the American Bar Association speaking with regard to the utilization of prehearing conferences by the Federal Communications Commission noted that the cases settled through this procedure demonstrate that:

> The new procedure is not without its defects and disadvantages. . . . For one thing, the new procedure requires and results in Examiners taking a more active and affirmative role in determining the areas of conflict between the parties and the evidence to be adduced as proof of them than heretofore thought necessary or desirable. This may result in *the substantial determination of a case in its early pleading stages rather than after the fullest hearing upon its complete merits.* . . . In addition, there is the very real danger that the concerted efforts to shorten hearings may, if not judiciously kept within reasonable bounds, lead to the denial of a full and fair hearing for one or more of the parties.
>
> As a major example thereof the Commission's repeated emphasis on the desirability of written evidence in order to speed the hearings has had a definite tendency to cause Examiners to cut down sharply on the oral presentation of testimony in comparative hearings, with the result that in some instances the parties' entire direct case may be required to be presented in writing and the appearance of witnesses may be limited to such cross-examination as is sought by opposing counsel.[96]

This Bar Association committee went on to add some traditional legal concepts to its interpretation of shortened procedure in the administrative process.

> . . . The growing limitation on witnesses' appearance and oral testimony eliminates one of the fundamental and long-established features of adjudicatory proceedings and takes away one of the material points of difference traditionally relied upon for a choice between contesting parties; i.e., credibility, particularly so here where character qualifications are so vital to the Commission decision. . . .
>
> It may rightfully be questioned whether proved and valuable legal procedures can be abandoned in order to satisfy the momentary needs of expediency without damaging the full and fair hearing required by due process and without

risking greater harm to the public interest than is sought to be avoided.[97]

In terms of common-law theory, the implications of the extensive limitation upon the formal administrative process are evident, for in fact the extent to which these forms of shortened procedure are successful results in depriving the formal hearing of any meaning. Within the common-law frame of reference it is doubtful that justice can be realized without traditional legal formalities.

Common-law doctrine, as manifested in the development of case law, and in the Administrative Procedure Act of 1946, requires that fundamental procedures of notice and hearing be followed by administrative agencies exercising adjudicative functions. Provisions of the APA, relative to formal adjudicative procedure, are operative only when such procedure is required by statute. In addition, such formal adjudicative procedure is not applicable in certain exempt areas.[98] Nevertheless, with respect to the ICC, the CAB, the SEC, the FCC, the NLRB, and the FTC, which have been subjected to examination in this chapter, the statutes under which these agencies operate require either that opportunity for hearing be given in certain cases or that hearings *must* be held in certain categories of cases, regardless of whether they are desired by the parties or the agency.

The agencies concerned, however, have not followed the paths of formal adjudicative procedure set out for them by statute; rather they have developed informal techniques which they have introduced into the formal adjudicative stage to expedite the hearing process. These techniques primarily consist of informal conferences and correspondence through which the agencies attempt to settle the case under consideration. The success of these informal techniques in effecting settlement of formal cases is so striking, in those administrative agencies that have been examined, that it is necessary to conclude that informal procedure is beginning to replace formal procedure, in the formal adjudicative stage itself. In other words, where informal procedure fails to prevent a case from reaching the formal administrative process, it is frequently successful in settling the case after appeal to the formal process has been taken. The informal techniques employed by these agencies vary, for example, from the ICC practice of requiring parties to submit their controversy to settlement through informal adjustment, on the one hand, to the general practice of using prehearing conferences of an informal nature to limit and define or settle issues before holding hearings. These conferences before hearings are frequently so successful that the hearing becomes essentially a formality, merely recording what has already been settled informally beforehand. Further, informal conferences are frequently employed during the course of the hearing. It is evident that administrative agencies are using informal techniques to aid adjudication wherever possible.

Although certain criticisms have been advanced against such extensive use of informal procedure in the formal administrative process, the prevailing opinion, on the part of the agencies, the parties coming under their jurisdiction, and the legal profession, seems to favor this method of settlement. Kenneth Culp Davis has noted that

> . . . the solution of the problem of determining when to require opportunity to be heard in the administrative process lies in discovering the best practical means in the varying circumstances for assuring enlightened administrative action which will protect those affected by considering their evidence and their argument and by letting them subject to their testing processes the materials on which the agency acts. Methods other than hearings are often most effective for this purpose; private interests frequently may be best protected by such methods as interviews, conferences, questionnaires, submission of tentative orders or regulations for written comments, collaboration between agency representatives and private representatives in drafting rules, consultation of agency officials with advisory groups which represent private parties, reception of written evidence and argument without an oral process." [99]

With regard to the ICC, Davis stated that "such devices as the ICC shortened and modified procedures are of vast significance and their further development and more extensive use should be encouraged." [100]

Finally, the implications of the use of shortened procedure by administrative agencies are evident. Davis has noted that "the prevailing judicial doctrine is that improper denial of administrative hearing may be remedied by availability of judicial review of sufficient scope, but widespread reliance upon this doctrine is unfortunate. Safeguards at the administrative stage are clearly superior to safeguards by a theoretical right of review which in practice is often illusory." [101] The question must necessarily be asked: What means can be employed to secure responsible action by administrative officials in this area where many cases are in fact not adjudicated by traditional common-law procedure but by informal means determined by each agency for itself? Because of the widespread use of informal procedure in the formal administrative process, it is no longer possible to say that private parties subject to the jurisdiction of administrative agencies have recourse to traditional adjudicative procedure to settle their cases.

Chapter III

APPLICATION CASES

Having discussed the use of informal techniques in the formal hearing stage, it is now necessary to analyze informal administrative settlement of cases before that stage is reached. One of the most important areas of informal settlement consists of administrative adjudication of applications for various types of licenses, certificates of public convenience and necessity, and benefits, as well as for other forms of permission to engage in particular activities. Adjudicative decisions made in this area are not only of vital concern to the parties making application, but to the community as a whole which in many instances is directly affected by the type of decision made. For example, such decisions determine the type of transportation facilities a particular community will have, the nature and number of radio and television stations that will serve the community, rates that may be charged for various services, as well as the type of protection the public will receive against illegal activity against the public interest. These decisions affect a large number of people and substantial property interests.

This chapter will include, first, an examination of the Administrative Procedure Act of 1946 in relation to the informal process, as this is the only general statutory control that exists in this area; second, the significance of informal adjudication of application cases will be illustrated through reference to a selected number of agencies.

THE ADMINISTRATIVE PROCEDURE ACT OF 1946

Various sections of the Administrative Procedure Act of 1946 relate to informal administrative adjudication. First, with regard to "every case of adjudication required by statute to be determined on the record after opportunity for an agency hearing,"[1] the Administrative Procedure Act provides that:

The Agency shall afford all interested parties opportunity

for (1) the submission and consideration of facts, argument, offers of settlement, or proposals of adjustment where time, the nature of the proceeding, and the public interest permit and (2) to the extent that the parties are unable so to determine any controversy by consent, hearing, and decision upon notice and in conformity with sections 7 and 8.[2]

In this instance the APA recognizes the importance of informal disposition, even though the parties are entitled by statute to a hearing.

Section 6(a) of the APA provides that:

Any person compelled to appear in person before any agency or representative thereof shall be accorded the right to . . . counsel. . . . So far as the orderly conduct of public business permits, any interested person may appear before any agency or its responsible officers or employees for the presentation, adjustment, or determination of any issue, request, or controversy in any proceeding (interlocutory, summary, or otherwise) or in connection with any agency function. Every agency shall proceed with reasonable dispatch to conclude any matter presented to it except that due regard shall be had for the convenience and necessity of the parties. . . .

This section adds to informal proceedings before administrative agencies the right to counsel. It further extends the informal process to a broader field than section 5(b), noted above, provides for reasonable dispatch, and requires the agencies to take into account the convenience and necessity of the parties.

If informal settlement fails in accordance with section 6(a) of the APA, section 6(d) becomes operative which provides that:

Prompt notice shall be given of the denial in whole or in part of any written application, petition, or other request of any interested person made in connection with any agency proceeding. Except in affirming a prior denial or where the denial is self-explanatory, such notice shall be accompanied by a simple statement of procedural or other grounds.

With respect to administrative power to license, section 9(b) of the APA states that:

. . . Except in cases of willfulness or those in which public health, interest, or safety requires otherwise, no withdrawal,

suspension, revocation, or annulment of any license shall be
lawful unless, prior to the institution of agency proceedings
therefor, facts or conduct which may warrant such action
shall have been called to the attention of the licensee by
the agency in writing and the licensee shall have been accorded opportunity to demonstrate or achieve compliance
with all lawful requirements.

Agency action in this respect amounts to informal adjudication.

With regard to judicial review of informal administrative determinations the APA provides that a reviewing court shall set
aside action found to be "unwarranted by the facts to the extent
that the facts are subject to trial de novo by the reviewing
court." [3] Any facts are subject to such review where they are
relevant to pertinent issues of law.[4] Francis E. Walter, chairman
of the House subcommittee in charge of the APA, noted that:
"Where there is no statutory administrative hearing to which
review is confined, the facts pertinent to any relevant question of
law must of course by tried and determined de novo by the reviewing court." [5] Given these considerations, it would appear
that the APA provides for judicial review of informal adjudicative decisions.

Finally, in commenting upon these provisions in the APA relating to informal administrative adjudication, Ashley Sellers
stated:

> Why is virtually an entire section of the statute given to
> informal rule-making, while no section or subsection ex-
> pressly applies to informal adjudication? The reason would
> appear to be, simply, that a statutory right and form of in-
> formal rule-making procedure had to be largely invented
> and hence was given a section of its own. Informal adjudica-
> tions, on the other hand, have long been an established (al-
> though perhaps complex, fragmentary, and sometimes un-
> certain) phase of administrative law as applied by the
> federal courts so that it was more convenient to follow the
> general structure of the existing law in that respect with
> no more than the addition of such amplifying and clarifying
> provisions as are to be found in sections 6(a), 6(d), and
> 10(e)(6).[6]

In summary, the Administrative Procedure Act encourages the

administrative utilization of informal adjudication even where an agency hearing may be required by law. Further, the APA outlines certain safeguards to protect private parties from completely arbitrary action in cases of informal adjudication. Finally, the APA appears to provide for limited judicial review of informal determinations, although this question is still unsettled.

THE SECURITIES AND EXCHANGE COMMISSION

The Securities and Exchange Commission administers, among others, the Securities Act of 1933,[7] the Securities Exchange Act of 1934,[8] the Public Utility Holding Company Act of 1935,[9] the Trust Indenture Act of 1939,[10] the Investment Company Act of 1940,[11] and the Investment Advisers Act of 1940.[12] Under these acts numerous persons and corporations must obtain the permission of the SEC before engaging in various forms of activity vital to them in the conduct of their business. Application cases constitute a large segment of the Commission's business.

The Securities Act of 1933 requires the Commission to disclose the facts with regard to securities that are to be sold in interstate or foreign commerce or through the mails. No securities can be sold in interstate or foreign commerce without proper registration. In appraising the soundness of a particular security the Commission can and does take into account the quality of the management of the firm, its general financial condition, and any other factors which might affect the worth of the security. The importance of this adjudicative power to the party registering a security for sale is evident.

The purpose of the Securities Exchange Act of 1934 is to prevent unfair practices on securities exchanges and over-the-counter markets. This act requires the registration of national securities exchanges as well as of brokers and dealers engaged in over-the-counter business. Further, all securities that are to be traded on such exchanges, unless exempted by the Commission, must be registered, and prescribed conditions of disclosure must be met by the registrant. The act gives the Commission broad powers of supervision with regard to exchanges, brokers and dealers, including those who trade securities on national exchanges.

The sanctions employed by the Commission in the administration of these acts are varied and effective. The staff of the Attorney General's Committee on Administrative Procedure noted:

> . . . many of the sanctions are complementary as well as cumulative. For example, if a person wilfully makes untrue or misleading statements in a registration statement filed under the Securities Act, the following consequences are possible: (1) the Commission may refuse to register the security or may issue a stop or refusal order; (2) further dealing in such security may be enjoined; (3) the registrant may be criminally prosecuted; and (4) the registrant and others who participated with him are civilly liable. If the underwriter is responsible for the misstatements and is a registered broker or dealer (1) his registration is subject to revocation; and (2) he is required to be expelled from a national securities association. If the false statement in a registration is not wilful, a stop or refusal order, or an injunction, as well as civil liability, may result; if a stop or refusal order issues, any person using the mails or the channels of interstate commerce to sell the security is subject to criminal prosecution or injunction, and, if such person is a registered broker or dealer he is subject to the various expulsions and revocations just described.[13]

Because of the implications of these Commission sanctions, which are as effective today as they were when the Attorney General's Committee wrote them, compliance is usually secured.

The Public Utility Holding Company Act of 1935 requires holding companies to register with the Commission, and in accordance therewith to supply certain information. A holding company must register in order to conduct business, for all channels of interstate commerce are closed to unregistered companies. The Commission must pass upon proposed security sales of holding companies and plans for reorganization, merger, or consolidation. Further, any sale of assets must be approved by the Commission. Commission decisions with respect to applications in these categories are of vital importance to the companies under consideration.

Finally, applications must be approved by the Commission in the administration of the Investment Company Act of 1940 and the Investment Advisers Act of 1940. The former regulates investment companies in the interest of investors; and in accordance with this, companies must register with the Commission and supply certain designated information. Under the latter act professional investment advisers must register, and are subject to the general supervision of the Commission to protect investors from fraud.

SEC Use of Informal Procedure

The SEC has noted in its Statement of Procedure that "the statutes and the published rules, regulations and forms thereunder prescribe the course and method of formal procedure to be followed in Commission proceedings. These are supplemented where feasible by certain informal procedures designed to aid the public and facilitate the execution of the Commission's functions." [14]

In describing its informal procedure the Commission notes that informal methods mostly concern the rendering of advice on the part of the Commission's staff to the public coming under its jurisdiction. In this regard the Commission has stated that:

> While opinions expressed by members of the staff do not constitute an official expression of the Commission's views, they represent the views of persons who are continuously working with the provisions of the statute involved. . . . In certain instances an informal statement of the views of the Commission may be obtained. The staff . . . will generally present questions to the Commission which involve matters of substantial importance and where the issues are novel or highly complex, although the granting of a request for an informal statement by the Commission is entirely within its discretion. [15]

It should be noted here that there is a Commission presumption of *expertise* on the part of its staff which causes it to attach a certain finality to staff interpretations of the law.

More specifically, the Commission staff gives interpretative and advisory assistance to:

> members of the general public, prospective registrants, applicants and declarants. For example, persons having a question regarding the availability of an exemption may secure

informal administrative interpretations of the applicable statute or rule as they relate to the particular facts and circumstances presented. Similarly, persons contemplating filings with the Commission may receive advice in the preparation thereof, including information as to the forms to be used and the scope of the items contained in the forms. . . . In addition, informal discussions with members of the staff may be arranged whenever feasible.[16]

In this way the staff of the SEC is able to adjust informally any differences that might exist between the parties filing and the Commission. Such procedure saves time and expense, in the interest of both the Commission and those coming under its jurisdiction.

Further, applications and other items requiring formal Commission action are examined by the appropriate section of the SEC with a view to correcting, beforehand, any variance between the item which will come before the Commission and applicable statutory standards and Commission rules. The filing party is notified of any such deficiencies.[17]

Informal procedure is utilized by the Commission *after* an application has been filed as well as before. In this area:

After the staff has had an opportunity to study an application or declaration, interested persons may informally discuss the problems therein raised to the extent that time and the nature of the case permit (e.g. consideration is usually given to whether the proceeding is contested and if so to the nature of the contest). In such event, the staff will, to the extent feasible, advise as to the nature of the issues raised by the filing, the necessity of any amendments to the documents filed, the type of evidence it believes should be presented at the hearing and, in some instances, the nature, form, and contents of documents to be submitted as formal exhibits. The staff will, in addition, generally advise as to Commission policy in past cases which dealt with the same subject matter as the filing under consideration.[18]

In this instance informal adjudication enters the formal administrative process if a hearing is deemed necessary.[19] The use of informal procedure, both before and after an application is made, conforms to the Commission's practice of employing informal techniques at every possible juncture in a proceeding.

Informal interpretative advice has been used by the Commission from its inception. In its first Annual Report the Commission stated that the Securities acts of 1933 and 1934 comprehend within their scope "such a variety of complex situations that innumerable questions necessarily arise . . . as to the applicability of the text of the law to situations which are not the subject of specific provision. . . ." [20] At that time, numerous advisory opinions were rendered with regard to various aspects of the '33 and '34 acts. The opinions given by letter or conference were classified and indexed to secure some consistency of interpretation. In addition, "while for the most part advisory opinions rendered, in answer to inquiries received, were not published, a number of these opinions were publicly released in cases where the questions involved had been the subject of widespread interest and numerous inquiries." [21]

Informal interpretative advice aided the Commission as well as private parties. In the first year of its operation the SEC stated that "it is believed that the spirit of coöperation engendered between the public and the Commission through this interpretative service was of definite value. The Commission also benefited greatly from the information obtained through the correspondence and conferences incidental to the rendering of such service. From these sources much valuable information was obtained, on the basis of which existing regulations were improved and new regulations promulgated.[22] Informal adjudicative conferences complemented and aided the legislative work of the Commission.

As is evident, the need for informal advice and informal adjudicative decisions is increased in the operation of the SEC because of the complex nature of the subject matter coming under the Commission's jurisdiction. Further, as the staff of the Attorney General's Committee noted, the SEC is primarily engaged in granting privileges and permitting activities in an area where speed and timing are of the essence. Because of this "there must often be considerable departure from orthodox procedures and formal patterns. Where an underwriter's deadline must be met, or a favorable market caught, it is inevitable—and proper—that there be resort to what may be called the 'after-hours' method of decision. Staff members, and the commissioners, must be available for quick and informal decision; especially in questions of registration of securities, flexibility which permits of quick staff conferences, telephonic decisions, and the like, is necessary." [23]

Further, the Attorney General's staff noted the widespread Commission utilization of prefiling conferences, especially with regard to applications under the Holding Company Act. Conferences thus "shape the form and nature of such requests." [24] With respect to the operation of this type of informal conference in the administration of the Holding Company Act the Attorney General's staff stated:

> . . . under the Holding Company Act, the initial stimulus for filing an application may come from the Commission's staff itself . . . each group in the Utilities Division is assigned to a few utility systems over which they keep continuous watch; accordingly, the staff may deem it advisable for a particular company to enter into particular transactions, suggestions will be made, and application thereafter filed.[25]

In this manner the Commission will initiate the very case that it adjudicates. If the Commission does not itself initiate an application in the administration of the Holding Company Act, at least "the problems are discussed in detail and the issues are explained long before the application is filed. When filed, it reflects the plans mutually evolved by the staff and the applicant.[26] This type of procedure is in general use by the SEC today.

Registration Under the Securities Act of 1933
and the Securities Exchange Act of '34

The work of examining applications filed under the '34 Act is integrated with and follows the same procedural pattern as such work under the '33 Act. In the discussion that follows, the '33 Act will in general be taken as typical of both.

The Commission's Statement of Procedure provides that:

> Registration statements, proxy statements, letters of notification, periodic reports, applications for qualification of indentures, and similar documents filed with the Commission . . . are routed to the Division of Corporation Finance, which passes initially on the adequacy of disclosure and

recommends the initial action to be taken. If the filing appears to afford inadequate disclosure, as for example through omission of material information or through violation of accepted accounting principles and practices, the usual practice is to bring the deficiency to the attention of the person who filed the document by a letter from the Assistant Director assigned supervision over the particular filing, and to afford a reasonable opportunity to discuss the matter and make the necessary corrections. This informal procedure is not generally employed where the deficiencies appear to stem from a deliberate attempt to conceal or mislead or where the Commission deems formal proceedings necessary in the public interest.[27]

Note that the informal technique of bringing any deficiency in an application to the attention of the applicant in order to provide the filing party with an opportunity for correction is employed by the Commission in all types of application cases.

The SEC Division of Corporation Finance examines registration statements and prospectuses filed in accordance with the Securities Act of 1933. "If a registration statement presents problems of an oil and gas, mining, or engineering nature, appropriate technical experts on the staff coöperate with the examiner, accountant and attorney of the examining section in processing that document. Not infrequently the staff may have occasion to consult with other departments or agencies of the government. . . ."[28]

As was noted above, extensive prefiling assistance is available to the registrant, who has the opportunity to participate in a conference with SEC staff experts. In general, such conferences are for the purpose of clarifying and simplifying the technical filing requirements in order to prevent waste effort on the part of the registrant.[29]

With respect to the deficiency letter, the Commission has stated that:

if examination discloses any omission or incomplete statement of material fact or inaccuracy in the registration statement, the staff relies for enforcement mainly upon another informal procedure, that of sending the registrant a "letter of comment," which points out the inadequacies found upon

examination. Such letter is sent as soon as possible after the
statement is filed and affords an opportunity for the filing of
a correcting amendment before the indicated effective date
of registration. This device avoids the necessity for the Commission to exercise its little-used authority under section 8
of the Act to institute formal proceedings against the registration statement. While the statute does not specifically
authorize such a procedure, perhaps no other device adopted
in connection with the registration process has equal capacity to accomplish a common-sense administration of the
Act in a manner calculated to afford fair treatment to registrants and cause a minimum of interference with financing
plans.[30]

The deficiency letter is an informal device developed by the SEC
to meet the unique needs arising from the type of business and
the nature of the subject matter regulated.

With respect to the deficiency letter, or letter of comment, the
staff of the Attorney General's Committee noted in a statement
still accurate today that the letter points out to the registrant
"not that the representations in the statement are untrue or misleading, but simply that on the basis of the mass of data which
the Commission has on file, certain specified material appears to
be untrue and misleading or certain information required seems
to be omitted." [31] Through the use of this letter the Commission
can usually "shape the registration . . . or, if the amendments
themselves are unsatisfactory, through a series of such letters. In
fact, however, one or at the most two letters are usually sufficient
to obtain the desired corrections." [32]

The essential reason for the effectiveness of the deficiency letter stems from the fact that "securities proposed to be sold must
be offered at a desirable time, and . . . the public notice which
would precede decisive proceedings would make successful public sale difficult. . . ." [33] Such factors as these essentially force
the parties registering to submit their application to informal
adjustment.

In this same regard, it is vital to the private interest registering
a security under the Securities Act of 1933 to obtain Commission
assent to the acceleration of the effective registration date. Section 8(a) of the '33 Act provides that:

> If any amendment to any statement is filed prior to the effective date of such statement, the registration shall be deemed to have been filed when such amendment was filed; except that an amendment filed with the consent of the Commission, prior to the effective date of the registration statement, or filed pursuant to an order of the Commission, shall be treated as a part of the registration statement.

By this provision the Commission can accelerate the effective date of a registration statement by allowing all amendments to be made within one twenty-day period. Without the consent of the Commission a new twenty-day waiting period would begin with the introduction of each amendment, delaying the registration indefinitely. In general, it is important for a new security issue to be marketed as quickly as possible, since the issue is timed to gain advantage of a favorable market.

The power of the Commission under the '33 Act is increased with respect to acceleration because

> virtually *every* registration statement under the '33 Act is necessarily filed incomplete: the registrant leaves certain matters (for example, the offering price) to be filled in by amendment. When either completing, or correcting amendments are so submitted, they are almost always accompanied by a request for acceleration under section 8(a). The examining group which scrutinizes the registration statement as amended reports thereon and at the same time reports upon the request for acceleration. The determination is made without hearing and, except in rare instances where as a matter of grace the registrant has been permitted to confer with the Commission, the process is wholly internal.[34]

Because of this need to obtain the consent of the Commission on acceleration with respect to every application coming before it, the Commission's deficiency letter must be heeded by the registrant to a greater extent than would otherwise be necessary. It is important for the registrant not to offend the Commission in any way.

The Securities Exchange Act of 1934, which requires the registration of national securities exchanges and of securities traded on those exchanges, requires a thirty-day waiting period before registration becomes effective. Amendments filed in regard to registration statements automatically become effective with the statement, even though they may be filed after the statement. However, the '34 Act enables the Commission to shorten the thirty-day waiting period; therefore frequent requests for acceleration are made, and are determined by the Commission in the same manner as such requests under the '33 Act, without hearing. Among the more important reasons for requests for acceleration under the '34 Act is the need to coördinate registration under the '33 and '34 acts.

In addition, the '34 Act states that Commission may, "if it appears necessary or appropriate in the public interest, or for the protection of investors, defer the effective date of any such registration as thus amended until the thirtieth day of such amendment." [35] The decision of whether or not to defer is made without hearing by the Commission. It should be noted that the criteria of the "public interest" gives the Commission broad discretion in this area.

James Landis, noting the success of informal adjudication by the SEC stated:

> The major reforms in regard to underwriting practice, corporate disclosure, and accounting techniques that the Commission has brought about . . . are not of public record. The trend of decisional policy is not readily discoverable from the stop order opinions of the Commission. The nature of these reforms can only be found by an examination of the successive amendments made by issuers of securities prior to the effective date—amendments made in the hope that the corrected form of disclosure will avert the bringing of a proceeding.[36]

With respect to the implications of such informal sanctions as publicity, Landis felt that "in a situation such as this the cure for arbitrariness with regard to administrative action does not lie in the divorcement of the prosecutory and adjudicative functions of the administrative [agencies]. Checks upon arbitrariness here must lie within the administrative [process] itself." [37]

Case Study

It is instructive in the area of informal adjudication under the Securities acts to observe an actual case settled with respect to registration under the '33 Act. The Commission described a sample case as follows:

A company operating a life, health, and accident insurance business filed its first registration statement under the Securities Act of 1933 purporting to cover an issue of "Special Stock Debentures" to be offered in units of $500 each. It appeared to the staff upon examination of the statement that these securities were not debentures at all . . . but were essentially contracts for the purchase of capital stock. Thus, the purchaser of the "debenture" agreed to pay $500 . . . and the company agreed in consideration thereof to deliver at the end of five years 25 shares of common capital stock. In each of these five years the purchaser was entitled to receive the equivalent of such dividends as would be paid on 25 shares of stock were such shares already issued; and he was entitled to an additional distribution based upon a percentage of the amount of life insurance renewal premiums paid to the company by its policy holders in each such year. The company referred to this latter distribution as a "bonus." Apart from making use of such misleading nomenclature as "debentures" and "bonus," the prospectus as originally filed was so prepared as to make it virtually impossible for even a skilled analyst to form a reasonable judgment of the investment merits of the securities.

In the ensuing examination process the prospectus and the security instrument itself were amended to substitute the term "Special Investment Contract" for "Special Stock Debenture"; and the term "bonus" which . . . did not appear to be applicable to any feature of these securities, was dropped.

To provide investors with some indication of what the purchaser's right to dividend equivalents might be worth, the amended prospectus also pointed out that earnings per share during the past four years had amounted to 30 cents, 62 cents, 12 cents, and 13 cents, respectively, and, to provide them with an indication of what the right to distributions based on the life insurance renewal premium business done by the company might be worth, it was furthermore pointed out . . . that, if the amount of such business done in 1950 were applied, total distributions over the five-year period would amount to some $28.14. It thus becomes apparent that, notwithstanding the specification in the investment contract that $25 of the $500 purchase price was to be attributed to the 25 shares of stock . . . and the remaining $475 was to be attributed to the rights to dividend equivalents and distributions based on life insurance renewal business, the cost of the stock should properly be regarded as very much greater than $25 ($1 per share). In this connection the amended prospectus states . . . very substantial increases in earnings will be necessary if purchasers of the investment contracts are to enjoy a satisfactory return on the stock they will receive at the price they are paying.

The amended prospectus also introduces an explanation that, assuming eventual issuance of all of the stock . . . , the original incorporators will hold some 72 percent of the outstanding stock, for which they paid approximately $37,-500 . . . incoming investors . . . will receive only an 18 percent interest in the company in exchange for a total contribution of $1,200,000.

In addition, the amended prospectus discloses that one of the company's two largest stockholders has repeatedly borrowed substantial sums from the company and that a presently outstanding loan (originally $600,000 but at the date of the prospectus reduced to $378,000) admittedly was under-collateralized by about 50 percent. This stockholder, the amended prospectus further discloses, profited to the extent of some $59,000 on a $500 investment, in the sale of property to the company, and to the extent of some $15,000 in connection with the purchase by the company of the business of another insurance company.

Besides, the registrant was called upon to file very substantial amendments to the financial statements included in the registration statement proper. . . . Following discussions with the staff, the company filed financial statements which were appropriately amended to reflect generally accepted accounting principles, resulting in a reduction of 1950 reported net income from $124,000 to $33,000 (approximately) and a reduction of earned surplus as of December 31, 1950, from $231,000 to $102,000 (approximately).[38]

This case illustrates not only the technical nature of the subject matter the Commission deals with, but also the very substantial effect that amendments may have on the prospects of a successful issue as well as on the interests of the public. Moreover, it illustrates the fact that formal proceedings would not be appropriate to the settlement of a case regarding the content of a registration statement. It is up to the Commission, on the basis of its investigations, staff analysis, and technical knowledge, to determine the nature of the disclosure that is to be made with regard to a particular security registration statement. The registrant has little choice but to accept the point of view of the Commission and informally adjust the matters of controversy between the Commission and itself. Thus there is considerable room for Commission discretion in determining the nature and content of the disclosure.

Significance of Informal Adjudication

The significance of informal adjudication of registration statement applications, both in terms of the interest of the individual applicant and in terms of the public interest, can be visualized in the accompanying table, which contains the number and

SEC—REGISTRATIONS UNDER THE SECURITIES ACT OF 1933

Fiscal year	No. of statements	All registrations (amount)	Total for cash sale for account of issuers
		(Amounts in millions of dollars)	
1935	284	913	686
1937	840	4,851	3,635
1939	344	2,579	2,020
1941	313	2,611	2,081
1943	123	659	486
1945	340	3,223	2,715
1947	493	6,732	4,874
1949	429	5,333	4,204
1951	487	6,459	5,169
1953	593	7,507	6,326
1955	779	10,960	8,277
1957	860	14,624	12,019
1959	1,055	15,657	12,095
1961	1,507	19,070	14,115

SOURCE: SEC Annual Reports.

amount of registrations that have been effected by the Commission from 1935 to 1961.

It is evident from the table that although the number of registrations is relatively small under the '33 Act, the amounts involved are significant in terms of both the individual and the public interests at stake.

The fact that informal adjudication is almost exclusively used in effecting registration statements under the '33 Act can be observed in the accompanying table, which contains the number of

SEC—STOP ORDER PROCEEDINGS UNDER THE
SECURITIES ACT OF 1933

Year	Pending	Instituted	Issued
1957	7	10	8
1958	7	8	5
1959	7	13	6
1960	13	8	9
1961	9	3	6

SOURCE: SEC Annual Reports.

stop order proceedings instituted and issued by the Commission under section 8 of the Act, from 1957 to 1961.

It is evident from the contrast between the number of stop order proceedings and the number of effective registration statements, that over 99 per cent of these applications are adjudicated informally.

Another indication of the effectiveness of the Commission's informal procedure is the fact that the Commission rarely feels compelled to resort to the criminal or civil procedures of the courts for enforcement. Prior to 1956, the SEC instituted on the average fewer than 30 injunction cases a year. Since 1956, that number has approximately doubled.[39] Insofar as criminal proceedings are concerned, the number of cases varies from year to year, but there has never been the necessity of developing more than 60 such cases in any given year, and generally the number is significantly less than that.[40]

The paucity of public hearings in the administration of various acts is indicated in the accompanying table.

SEC—PUBLIC HEARINGS

Fiscal year	'33 Act	'34 Act	Holding Co. Act	Trust Ind. Act	Invest. Advisors Act	Invest. Co. Act
1950	1	24	71	0	1	1
1951	0	10	58	1	3	0
1952	2	14	46	1	1	7
1953	4	23	36	0	4	0
1954	4	26	14	0	0	2

SOURCE: SEC Annual Reports.

Here the figures for the years 1950 to 1954 have been taken, both because they are typical and because of the availability of statistics for those years. It can be seen that, except for the administration of the Holding Company Act, hearings are not an important device in aiding Commission decisions. As has been pointed out, even where hearings are held, especially in the case of the administration of the Holding Company Act, they are considerably modified and are frequently rendered meaningless through the use of informal techniques.

Summary

The operation of the Securities and Exchange Commission presents a vivid example of informal adjudication of application cases. The Commission is primarily concerned with approving, modifying, or disapproving numerous applications made to it under various statutes for privileges of one type or another. These applications are generally concerned with matters of technical complexity; and with regard to the Securities Act of 1933 and the Securities Exchange Act of 1934, it is imperative for the party making application to secure approval within a short period of time and without adverse publicity. These three factors combine to increase the need for and the effectiveness of informal methods of disposing of applications to the Commission. The informal techniques used by the Commission center, first, upon informal interpretative advice with respect to the legality and content of particular applications. Further, in this regard, the Commission frequently initiates applications itself in the administration of the Holding Company Act. These informal techniques are carried out through correspondence or conference with the applicant. Second, the Commission employs the device of the deficiency letter with respect to applications made under all of the acts it administers. The deficiency letter is simply a letter calling to the attention of the filing party any deficiency that exists, in the opinion of the Commission, in the application that has been submitted. The deficiency letter has proven particularly effective because of the needs of many registrants to market securities as quickly as possible, and to avoid adverse publicity that would result from any formal Commission action against a security issue. Also in this respect, the applicant must secure the Commission's consent to accelerate the effective date of the registration, thereby avoiding interminable delay which would otherwise result.

Because of these various factors it is evident that the device of the formal hearing has little use in the administration, by the SEC, of the various acts under its jurisdiction. Not only would formal procedure hamper the Commission by placing an impossible burden upon it but it would also cause injustice to the private parties coming under its jurisdiction by preventing expedition in the operation of their businesses, thus causing them to suffer the delay and expense that usually accompany formal proceedings. Since the safeguards against arbitrary exercise of power that are normally felt to be present in formal hearings have little meaning in the operation of the SEC, it is imperative, as Landis pointed out, to devise some *internal* method of securing administrative responsibility, specifically a method imposed by administrative officials upon themselves.

THE INTERSTATE COMMERCE COMMISSION

The Interstate Commerce Commission, in dealing with the railroad and trucking industries, has statutory power to grant or deny certain privileges with respect to the operation of these groups. Because of this it is necessary for the Commission to adjudicate application cases in various areas.

Motor Carrier Adjudication

First, with respect to the jurisdiction of the Commission under the Motor Carrier Act of 1935, any motor carrier wishing to engage in interstate or foreign commerce must procure a certificate of public convenience and necessity from the Commission before conducting any business. In order for motor carriers to sell transportation they must be able to demonstrate their ability to handle the transportation, and further demonstrate that their business is in the public interest and in accordance with the provisions of the Motor Carrier Act.

With respect to the early adjudication of these motor carrier applications for certificates of public convenience and necessity, the staff of the Attorney General's Committee noted that:

> The great bulk of the . . . applications are disposed of by methods which are wholly informal. After the application has been recorded and docketed in the Washington office . . . it is sent to one of the . . . field offices for investigation. The field office calls in the applicant and others who may have any interest in the application and determines by informal conferences whether or not the application should be granted. Applications are required by the Act to be made under oath and the task may consist in some cases of little more than a verification of the facts stated in the application. About 60% of all applicants are single truck operators, most of whom have no books of accounts or written records. Proofs may be made often by reference to old telephone directories, or to bank accounts or similar records, but much of the proof is frequently made simply by word of mouth. If the field office is satisfied of entitlement then a compliance order is issued.[41]

This is essentially the way the ICC operates today in this area. If protests are filed against the compliance order, once again informal methods are employed in the field in an attempt to satisfy the protestant and the applicant; however, a relatively large proportion of these cases reach the trial examiner level.

With regard to motor carriers, the Commission has jurisdiction over the substitution, transfer, or lease of operating rights. These applications are also adjudicated by the field office and, unless objections to granting an application are raised, the application is usually granted automatically. The Attorney General's staff noted in this respect that "financial statements, insurance, tariffs, and questions of duplication or splitting of service, must all be taken into account and some rather difficult questions of policy are often presented in these cases. These applications are handled wholly by informal methods. If an applicant takes exception to a denial of his application, he is accorded the opportunity for hearing, but never yet has a hearing been requested as a result of the denial of such an application." [42] In addition to these case categories, the Bureau of Motor Carriers must adjudicate several other types of cases.

The number of applications received by the Commission for certificates of public convenience and necessity of all types approximates 9,000 per year. Hearings, conducted by examiners, are held in about a third of these cases. The ICC feels strict formal procedure would unduly hamper expeditious settlement in this area.

ICC Tariff Cases

A second area in which the ICC illustrates the widespread use of informal techniques with respect to application cases is that of approving, rejecting, or suspending tariffs. Decisions in this field substantially affect the carriers directly concerned, as well as shippers and the general public. The Commission has stated, with regard to the filing of tariffs, that "except to the extent orders of the Commission may require carriers to maintain maximum or minimum rates, or rate relationships, the carriers are free to publish and file such rates as they believe to be lawful without prior approval of the tariff by the Commission. The carriers' representatives, however, do frequently consult informally with members of the Commission's staff . . . to obtain their views as to whether certain proposed tariff provisions would be considered as complying with the Commission's tariff regulations." [43] In this way the Commission's staff gives interpretative advice, and what in fact may be an adjudicative decision can result from such informal conferences.

In this area, the Commission, on its own initiative or because a complaint has been registered, can suspend the operation of the filed schedule for a maximum period of seven months, and order a formal hearing with respect to the lawfulness of a particular schedule. Whether or not to suspend, upon application, is determined by the Board of Suspension. The Commission's Rules of Practice provide, with respect to the operation of this Board, that "the proceedings . . . shall be informal. No transcription of such proceedings will be made. Subpoenas will not be issued and, except when applications or petitions are required to be attested, oaths will not be administered." [44]

With respect to suspension proceedings of the ICC during the 'thirties the Attorney General's staff noted that after suspension orders were issued the case was nevertheless settled in some instances before formal proceedings began. In this regard "the Chairman of the Board of Suspension, or the Director of the Bureau of Traffic, in some cases constitutes himself a mediator and attempts to effect a settlement through conference or correspondence with the parties." [45] Today, conferences in this area have been found very useful, and frequently after such a conference the suspension order is vacated or modified. Finally, in this regard, informal conferences are frequently held before the order is issued, between the members of the Board of Suspension and representatives of carriers and complainants.

Suspension cases may also be discontinued before going to formal hearing "because the respondent carrier decides to cancel the suspended matter rather than go to hearing and attempting to justify the lawfulness of the suspended schedules." [46] Such discontinuance may, of course, reflect an informal understanding between the Commission and the parties to the dispute.

A further informal technique used by the Commission to aid in adjudication of tariff applications is the device of criticizing tariff publications, although allowing them to stand. The purpose of such criticism is "to obtain compliance with the Commission's rules governing the construction and filing of tariffs. The criticism, therefore, serves to require correction of the publication that is criticized as well as to avoid similar departures from the rules in schedules that are filed in the future." [47] Such a device

governs the procedure of filing tariffs more than their content.
The table illustrates the number of tariff applications received

ICC TARIFF APPLICATIONS AND REJECTIONS

Year	Applications	Rejections
1957	186,610	2,310
1958	191,997	2,748
1959	193,063	3,351
1960	187,849	3,151
1961	204,275	4,057

SOURCE: ICC Annual Reports.

and rejected by the Commission during the years 1957 to 1961.

This table illustrates both the large number of tariff applications filed with the Commission, and the small number of rejections, indicating that most applications are approved automatically. In any event, formal procedure is not used in either the approval or rejection process.

The accompanying table indicates, for the years 1957–1961,

ICC TARIFF CRITICISMS AND SUSPENSION PROCEEDINGS

Year	Tariff publications criticized	Rate adjustments protested and suspension asked	Suspension proceedings instituted	Suspension without hearing*
1957	9,893	3,620	1,635	594
1958	8,060	4,532	2,236	878
1959	8,516	5,600	1,811	867
1960	16,599	4,252	1,281	541
1961	19,072	4,855	1,744	616

SOURCE: ICC Annual Reports.
   * Involving one or more rate adjustments.

the number of tariff publications criticized by the Commission; the number of such rate adjustments (tariff publications of course involve rate adjustments) that have been protested by various groups that ask the Commission to suspend the tariff;

the number of suspension proceedings instituted by the ICC; and finally the suspension proceedings disposed of without hearing.

The Commission has stated that the term "rate adjustments protested and suspension asked" refers to "adjustments, in tariff form, actually filed with the Commission and which have been protested. An adjustment may involve more than one tariff as where carriers in a given territory decide to establish a general increase in rates and charges. All of the tariffs proposing to establish that increase on a common effective date would be treated as one adjustment. On the other hand, if a particular change in rates is published in a single tariff, that would likewise constitute an adjustment." [48]

From the table it is evident that suspension proceedings are instituted in only a small number of cases where suspension is requested. In determining whether or not to institute suspension proceedings the Commission is engaged in an important form of adjudication. Again, no formal proceedings are used in this area, for "suspension and rejection of proposed schedules by the Commission are discretionary powers, and when the Commission declines to suspend or when a schedule is rejected no method is employed to gain acceptance of that fact." [49] These comments pertain to the rejection of schedules as well as to the suspension of tariff adjustments.

Fourth Section Applications

Finally, application cases arise under the jurisdiction of the ICC because, under section 4 of the Interstate Commerce Act, the Commission may grant relief from the provision stated there which requires carriers to provide the same rate for long and short hauls on the same line, and further provides that through rates must not be greater than the aggregate of the intermediate rates. Applications for such relief are known as "fourth section applications." The Fourth Section Board utilizes the same informal procedure as that employed by the Board of Suspension in reviewing these applications.[50] Formal hearings are virtually never conducted with respect to the adjudication of such applications. This fact can be seen in another table, which sets forth the number of Fourth Section applications received by the

Commission between 1950 and 1959, as well as the number of these applications which were heard.

ICC FOURTH SECTION APPLICATIONS

Year	Applications	No. heard	Year	Applications	No. heard
1950	905	338	1955	1,421	61
1951	984	33	1956	1,573	25
1952	984	52	1957	1,660	14
1953	1,093	13	1958	834	7
1954	1,244	21	1959	729	33

SOURCE: ICC Annual Reports.

From this table it is manifest that as the number of Fourth Section applications increased the number heard decreased. At the present time, approximately 5 per cent of these cases reach the hearing process of the Board, but of course that process is itself highly informal.

Summary

In most instances, it is clear, the adjudication of application cases by the Interstate Commerce Commission is carried out through the use of informal conferences or correspondence. In some cases, such as in the filing of tariff schedules, the Commission gives informal interpretative advice to applicants before filing takes place. In other instances, such as in the rejection of requests for suspension of a particular tariff schedule, or the rejection of the tariff application itself, the Commission does not employ formal proceedings of any type. Applications by motor carriers for certificates of public convenience and necessity, as well as many other types of applications handled by the Bureau of Motor Carriers, are more frequently than not adjudicated informally in the field. Unquestionably, one of the reasons for the extensive use of informal methods by the ICC is the fact that a considerable volume of applications is presented to it each year, and in order to accomplish its job in passing upon these applications it is necessary for the Commission to adopt informal techniques wherever possible. The Interstate Commerce Commission, like the Securities and Exchange Commission, illustrates the lack of use of formal proceedings in the adjudication of application cases. Because of the lack of powerful sanctions in the operation of the ICC in this area, the problem of administrative responsibility is not as acute as it is in the case of the SEC; however, the procedures used to pass upon certificates for public convenience and necessity, tariff schedules, suspension requests, and Fourth Section applications should be based upon defined standards, which in themselves may provide greater safeguards against the exercise of arbitrary power than formal adjudicative techniques.

THE FEDERAL COMMUNICATIONS COMMISSION

With respect to the general significance of the FCC a House Select Committee states:

> No over-all estimate of the money invested in the various industries regulated by the FCC ever has been made by an authoritative source . . . but it would be on the conservative side to say that the FCC has an important effect on an investment totaling literally tens of billions of dollars, in which millions of Americans have a stake.
>
> The physical properties of all radio and television stations, the telegraph and radio companies, the telephone companies, and other vast enterprises under its supervision are of incalculable worth to our nation in war and in peace. The investment of the telephone industry alone . . . surpasses . . . [24] billions of dollars.[51]

Volume and Scope of FCC Adjudication

This committee was in fact conservative in its assessment of the importance of the operations of the FCC. In 1959, the Commission related its activities of that year with those of 1934, the year of its establishment, in the following way:

> In the FCC's quarter century, these major events have transpired:
>
> Radio authorizations have practically multiplied by that number of years—from slightly more than 100,000 at the close of the Commission's first year to nearly 2.5 million today.
>
> Radio stations of all kinds have increased from 51,000 to

more than 507,000 and currently represent the use of about 1.8 million transmitters.

From 600 stations (all AM) in 1934, broadcast authorizations collectively today exceed 10,000, of which 3,500 are AM and over 970 and 930 are TV and FM, respectively.

The number of broadcast receivers has soared from 18½ million to more than 200 million (150 million aural and 50 million TV). Almost two-thirds of the world's total are in the United States. This country now has more sets than people and almost three times as many sets as it has automobiles.

Amateur radio operator authorizations have climbed from about 36,000 to around 188,000.

Commercial radio operator permits have skyrocketed from some 21,000 to more than 1.7 million.

. . . Personalized use of radio, impossible until 1949 except by amateurs, is presently reflected in more than 50,000 citizens radio operations.[52]

In addition to the regulation of these areas, the FCC controls "common carriers" such as telephone and telegraph companies. In all of these areas the Commission must approve applications for the particular radio operation requested. Informal adjudication of such applications is of vital significance both to the public and to the FCC.

In 1934, the Commission received less than 10,000 applications for adjudication. In 1961, close to 700,000 applications had to be processed, as indicated in the accompanying table.

FCC APPLICATION CASES (1961)

Class	Number
1. Broadcast services (nonhearing)	12,613
2. Safety and special services	350,177
3. Common carrier services	5,612
4. Experimental	1,369
5. Commercial radio operators	329,744
Total	699,515

SOURCE: 1959 FCC Annual Report.

All of these applications are adjudicated informally. In contrast to this large volume of informal cases, the FCC in 1961 designated a grand total of 554 cases of all types for hearing. At the beginning of the 1961 fiscal year there were 794 docketed cases pending, and of these 369 were disposed of without hearing. Only 316 hearing cases were decided by the FCC in 1959.[53] This remarkable contrast should not go unnoticed.

Informal Decision-Making

As indicated above, applications are required in all of the diverse areas over which the Commission has jurisdiction, such as operator and station licenses, construction permits or their modification, and so on.[54] In most instances the form and content of applications are carefully prescribed by the FCC. In a limited number of cases informal applications may be made.[55] In addition to having jurisdiction over various types of application cases, the Commission requires the submission of numerous kinds of financial reports, contracts relating to certain areas, reports relating to station ownership, and so on.[56] The information in these reports must conform to Commission standards.

Applications that do not conform with the requirements of a procedural nature established by the Commission may be dismissed. Only "complete" applications are accepted for filing.[57] Further, any applications may be dismissed without prejudice, as a matter of right, prior to the designation of such application for hearing.[58] Needless to say, a significant degree of adjudication takes place in the process of determining whether or not to accept an application for consideration.

Three steps in the process of institutional decision-making are followed by the FCC upon acceptance of an application. First, the complete application file is sent to the FCC engineering division, where the application is reviewed from an engineering standpoint. This group then prepares a draft report containing its recommendations with respect to the adjudication of the application.[59] Second, the complete file is sent to the accounting division, where recommendations are prepared regarding the application from an accounting standpoint.[60] Finally, the legal department reviews the complete file, which contains the recommendations of both the engineering and the accounting divisions, for the purpose of determining "whether the authorization requested will be in accordance with the Commission's policies, rules and regulations, and any other requirements imposed by law." [61] A joint report is prepared and the matter is then placed on the agenda of the Commission.

In general, if the Commission finds upon examination of an application file presented to it by its legal department that the public interest, convenience, and necessity will be served by granting the application, it will be granted subject to protest.[62] Otherwise the case will be designated for hearing; however, even after the case has been assigned to hearing the issues may be settled informally.[63]

Applications cannot be granted without hearing unless it is evident that the applicant is legally, technically, and financially qualified, which is determined respectively by the legal, engineering, and accounting divisions. In order for an application to be granted without hearing it cannot affect licenses already in existence.[64] Needless to say, the determination of these conditions is within the discretion of the Commission. Finally, with regard to applications for the operation of television stations, hearings are required only where channels being requested coincide.[65]

Provision for bypassing formal procedure is also present with respect to applications for broadcasting facilities. If such applications have been designated for hearing "the parties may request the Commission to grant or deny the application upon the basis of the information contained in the application and other papers . . . without the presentation of oral testimony." [66] Such a procedure saves time and expense for both the Commission and the parties involved.

With regard to Commission revocation of licenses, show-cause or cease-and-desist orders are made. The person or institution involved is entitled to a hearing, but it can be waived.[67] This is also true with respect to Commission modification of licenses and suspension of operator licenses.[68]

It is evident from the preceding examination of the Commission's procedure in the adjudication of application cases that every opportunity is taken to settle issues without recourse to formal proceedings. As a general rule, applications are adjudicated informally through the institutional decision-making process described. This extensive reliance upon informal procedure has long been typical of FCC operations, as is indicated by the remarks of the staff of the Attorney General's Committee on Administrative Procedure in 1941.[69] They noted that although opportunity for hearing was theoretically present in many types of cases, rarely was it necessary for the Commission to utilize a formal hearing process because of the successful use of informal procedure.[70]

For example, with regard to the suspension of operators' licenses, similar procedures existed in 1940 and 1962.[71] The Attorney General's staff stated relevant to this adjudicative field that:

> It is rare indeed that an operator requests a hearing on the matter. Because the Commission does not hold hearings in the field, it is necessary for the operator to come to Washington to defend himself, a course which he is quite unlikely to be able to pursue. It redounds to the Commission's credit . . . that the greatest care is taken by the Field Section and the Law Department before suspension orders are recommended. The members of the staff are fully cognizant that their word is sufficient to deprive a man of his livelihood. . . .
>
> In order to minimize the possibility of error in these matters, the attempt is always made by the field inspector investigating the case to interview the operator before reporting the matter to Washington. In many cases confessions are obtained from operators, together with explanations of their unlawful activities. If the operator cannot be reached by the field inspector, the Law Department invariably attempts to communicate with him before arriving at its recommendation.[72]

In this area informal conferences and correspondence have replaced a formal hearing procedure which could not in fact work effectively.

The Commission has also carried out the suspension or revocation of amateur licenses through informal techniques throughout its history. The amateur, like the commercial operator, must pass FCC examinations for a license. Amateur, like commercial license applications, must be designated for hearing; however, in the case of amateur applications hearings have seldom been held "because the applicant realizes that he will be unable to maintain the burden of proof on the designated issues or because the expense entailed by a hearing is too great to warrant the applicant's availing himself of the opportunity to be heard." [73] Of course expense has always been more of a hindrance to amateur operators in the utilization of formal procedure than it would be to commercial operators, for the latter have both a monetary stake in obtaining a license and greater resources.

With respect to the reluctance of the FCC to hold hearings in the area of application cases, some very revealing testimony was given by the chairman of the Commission, George C. McConnaughey, before the House Antitrust Subcommittee of the Committee on the Judiciary in 1957. The case under discussion involved an $8.5 million station transfer, which was subject to FCC approval. The following exchange took place:

> Mr. Keating . . . When you are determining whether or not to hold a hearing do you lean toward holding one or against one before you reach a decision?
> Mr. McConnaughey . . . I think lean against it.
> Mr. K. What I am getting at is if I were sitting in your position I think I would lean toward it. You say you lean against it. I assumed that it is relatively unusual to take such particularly important action as this without a hearing. Am I wrong in that?
> Mr. M. You are, yes, sir. I think the statutory construction is . . . to lean against having a hearing.
>
> Mr. K. Could counsel point out to me what section?
> Mr. Baker. If you compare the Communications Act with any other regulatory statute most other agencies cannot grant or deny a license for anything without a hearing. The FCC has to make certain findings and go through many formal proceedings before it can initiate a hearing.
> Those were amendments put into section 309. I think their legislative history would indicate that because of the volume of the many matters relating to communications, the Congress felt the normal process should be to

grant licenses and approvals without hearings. Only in exceptional circumstances where it seems necessary, in fact where the Commission might conclude that it should deny the grant is a hearing anticipated. . . .

You can't say, "Well, we think we want a hearing here." You must write them a formal letter telling them everything that you think may prevent you from making a finding that is in the public interest. Then they must be given an opportunity to answer these questions . . . then you must again consider whether you can grant without a hearing. . . . I think in that context you would have to say that this as compared, for example, with the Civil Aeronautics Act implies that the normal process is to grant without a hearing.

Mr. Keating. That comes as a great surprise to me. How many transactions comparable to this $8½ million transaction do you have a year in the FCC?

Mr. McConnaughey. Three or four or five. . . .

Mr. K. . . . This was the largest one you ever had.

Mr. M. I think that is right. . . .

There were 25 to 30 of these transfers [each month] . . . varying in size. Some of them have been very substantial. . . .

I haven't been in the Commission a long time. *I don't know whether there have ever been any hearings or not.*

Mr. K. In other words hearings are relatively infrequent.

Mr. M. Extremely, almost nonexistent . . . on a sale and transfer of a license.[74]

It is evident from the above passage that the use of hearings by the FCC in regard to application cases is rare indeed, so rare in the category of transferring and selling licenses that the Chairman of the Commission himself could not recall whether or not any hearings had been held in the past. The statute conferring power upon the Commission, as well as the Commission itself, discourage formal hearing procedure.

The NBC—Westinghouse Case

The case involved in the above discussion before the Antitrust Subcommittee concerned the approval by the FCC of the trans-

fer and sale of an important television station owned by Westinghouse, with an NBC affiliation, to the National Broadcasting
Company in exchange for certain NBC stations plus a payment
of $3 million. Serious issues were raised with respect to the de-
velopment of a monopoly by NBC, and with respect to whether
or not NBC used the threat of withdrawal of its affiliation from
the Westinghouse station, which would ruin the station, in order
to force Westinghouse to sell. The station itself was valued at
$8.5 million. The Commission adjudicated the application for
this transfer and sale without holding a hearing.

Commissioner Bartley dissented from the opinion of the Commission, in this case, stating that he felt that a hearing should
have been held.

> I am of the opinion that the Commission should designate
> these applications for hearing upon appropriate issues, de-
> signed to obtain a full and complete disclosure on the record
> of all the facts concerning the questions and matters set
> forth below, so that the Commission will thereafter have an
> adequate factual basis upon which to reach a determination
> as to whether these transfers will, in fact, serve the public
> interest, convenience, and necessity.[75]

Commissioner Doerfer effectively answered Bartley when,
speaking for the majority, he noted:

> The dissenting opinion strongly urges the necessity for a
> full hearing upon appropriate issues designed to obtain a
> complete disclosure on the record of all the views concern-
> ing the questions which have been raised. All questions sub-
> mitted have been answered. A complete disclosure of all
> relevant facts has been frankly made.
>
> Unless the Commission is of a view that all of the relevant
> and material facts . . . can be obtained by no other means
> than a formal hearing, a hearing is not required. . . . A
> summary of the interviews and the answers to written inter-
> rogatories indicates that no question propounded remains
> unanswered. . . . All that could possibly be achieved by a
> formal hearing was obtained through the investigatory proc-
> ess. The prime function of a hearing is to determine issues
> of fact or of law. The matter is ripe for decision. . . . If

additional facts were deemed material, no reason appears why they cannot be obtained by furtherance of the investigatory process. The answers received, as suggested by the staff, appear to be more frank and illuminating than would be the case if pried out of witnesses in the atmosphere of a formal hearing. . . . Administrative law has been woven into American jurisprudence primarily upon the theory that it would provide expeditious handling of matters involving Government policy as well as an efficient and economical process of ascertaining the basic facts. Investigation—especially in nonadversary matters—is a useful and efficient tool in the prompt disposition of administrative matters.[76]

Although this case was nonadversary, in the sense that no controversy appeared to exist between the parties submitting the application, an important case did exist between the Commission as a representative of the "public interest" and the applicants. Some members of the Commission's staff felt that a restraint of trade, as defined by the anti-trust laws, would result if the sale was not blocked; hence it was necessary for the FCC to apply whatever standards it had developed in this area to the case at hand. In this respect the Commission itself became a party.

The FCC and Tariffs

Having discussed the adjudicative procedure of the FCC with regard to various types of application cases, another significant case category, tariff filings, will be examined briefly. Telephone and telegraph companies, in addition to the numerous applications they must file with the FCC concerning the various services they wish to provide customers, must also secure Commission approval of their rates. Action in this area profoundly affects the public, as well as the companies themselves. In a typical year the FCC receives approximately 16,000 applications for rate adjustments, in addition to the application case load noted above.[77] In this area, as in others, the Commission has traditionally relied upon informal procedure to adjust any disputes that arise. In 1941 the Attorney General's Committee staff noted that when the FCC had to resort to suspension proceedings in the tariff field "no attempt is made to adjust the controversy with the carrier

prior to the service of the suspension order. So far as can be
ascertained, in almost every case in which the Commission has
suspended a schedule, the carrier withdrew the objectionable
schedule and no hearing was necessary." [78] Where less drastic
action was taken by the Commission, rates could be adjusted
informally to conform to policy standards. Today, as in the past,
the FCC adjusts cases in this field through informal procedure.

Summary

The extraordinary scope of the FCC's activities has been noted.
Application cases constitute the most significant part of the Commission's business. In the course of adjudicating these cases the
FCC affects in a very substantial way not only the individual
applicants but also the general public. These decisions determine
the quantity, and to some extent the quality, of radio and television service for the nation, as well as telephone and telegraph
rates in interstate and foreign commerce. As a general rule, virtually all of the more than half a million application cases determined by the Commission each year are adjudicated through
an informal institutional decision-making process, which is particularly emphasized because of the technical nature of the subject matter upon which decisions must be based. Further, the
majority of those few cases that are designated for hearing are
settled without hearing, reflecting consent on the part of the
parties involved to informal adjustment of the controversy.
Among the informal techniques used correspondence and conferences are the most important methods of disposition. The
Commission itself has expressed the belief that the necessary
information for arriving at most decisions can be gained more
effectively through utilization of staff investigations than through
reliance upon formal hearing procedure. The Federal Communications Commission procedure manifests the same tendency, evident in the SEC and the ICC which have been discussed previously, to discard formal adjudicative procedure and rely upon
informal techniques to make adjudicative decisions. The same
urgent problems regarding administrative responsibility raised
with respect to the SEC and the ICC are present in the operations of the FCC in the area of application case adjudication.

THE NATIONAL LABOR RELATIONS BOARD

Although the National Labor Relations Board is primarily concerned with cases arising from complaints, it is charged under the National Labor Relations Act with the determination of the "appropriate" bargaining unit.[79] Under this Act the Board was to determine upon petition by one or more labor organizations for recognition: (1) will the unit (employer, craft, or plant) insure the employees "the full benefit of their right to self-organization and to collective bargaining"?[80] and (2) have the majority of employees within the unit named a collective bargaining representative? This provision necessitates the adjudication of application cases by the Board.

The Labor Management Relations Act of 1947[81] extended such representation (application) cases to: (1) employees desiring to decertify their union because of its unrepresentative character; (2) employer's petitions where only one union is seeking recognition as the collective bargaining agent of the petitioner's employees. Previously the Board entertained an employer's petition only when two or more labor organizations were contending for recognition as bargaining agent.

Further, the Labor Management Relations Act of 1947 provides for Board certification of union-shop agreements. If a labor union has been certified as legal representative of the employees, then it may petition for a union-shop agreement, whereupon the Board conducts an election, and if 30 per cent or more of the employees are in favor of the union shop such an agreement can be put into effect. However, in this type of case no question of representation arises, and usually the case "is disposed of by consent election and does not come before the Board for decision, for there is no question to be determined, except the single one that the employees themselves decide at the polls."[82] In fact, then, no adjudicative decision is made in this area, for the employees themselves make the decision by vote.

Informal Settlement Procedures

With respect to the adjudication of these applications requesting designation as bargaining representative, the staff of the

Attorney General's Committee noted that, although section 9(c) of the National Labor Relations Act stated that in these cases the Board "shall provide for an appropriate hearing upon due notice . . . ," the Board nevertheless developed informal adjudicative procedures to handle such cases. When an application is received a preliminary examination is conducted by a field examiner to ascertain certain facts with regard to the unit desiring recognition. If, after investigation, it is determined that the applicant does not command a majority of the employees' unit under consideration, or that the applicant does not represent an appropriate bargaining unit, the field examiner requests that the application be withdrawn. The Attorney General's staff noted in this respect that

> refusal to withdraw, under these circumstances, is generally followed by the dismissal of the petition. It is frequently possible to arrange a settlement of the controversy, or, to be more accurate, to avoid the necessity for formal proceedings, by the employment of the conference method. Adjustments take the form of outright recognition of the petitioning union by the employer, or the determination of the question of representation either by checking the union members' cards against the employer's payroll or by holding a consent election.[83]

If the application is accepted, and if a controversy exists, informal adjudicative techniques are employed by the Board. It is evident that the Board has relied upon informal procedure from the very beginning.

The use of a consent election agreement device to secure informal adjustment of a particular application case was developed by the Board under the Wagner Act. This procedure was incorporated into the Taft-Hartley Act by section 9(c)(4) which authorizes "the waiving of hearings by stipulation for the purpose of a consent election in conformity with regulations and rules of decision of the Board." [84] The Board provides for two types of agreements in this area: "(1) consent election agreement, followed by Regional Director's determination, and (2) consent election agreement, followed by Board determination." [85]

These agreements are:

> identical insofar as the pre-election phase of the proceeding

is concerned; each fixes by consent the unit of employees appropriate for collective bargaining, the payroll period for determining the eligibility of the voters, the time and place of the election, and other details pertinent to the balloting. The settlement of these issues by agreement dispenses with the need for time-consuming formal procedure consisting of notice, hearing, findings of fact, conclusions of law, and direction of election by the Board. The election can therefore be held with dispatch and its result is normally accepted by all—employees, employers, and contending unions—as a fair and final determination of which union, if any, is authorized to act as the employees' representative.[86]

This informal technique combines the use of informal conferences to settle certain basic issues, with elections which determine the union that will be certified as bargaining agent.

If disputed questions arise during the course of an election, the Board type of agreement provides for formal decision by the Board.[87] "Thus, the essence of this agreement is that the consent phase ceases with the settlement of the preelection arrangements and the steps thereafter are contested by the parties with final decision resting in the Board." [88]

On the other hand, "the regional director type of agreement retains its consent character throughout. This agreement invests in the Regional Director . . . conclusive authority to resolve disputes raised by the election." [89] Under the Board's Statement of Procedure "this form of agreement provides that the rulings of the Regional Director on all questions relating to the election (for example, eligibility to vote and the validity of challenges and objections) are final and binding." [90] In this way, the process of informal adjustment of any controversy that might exist can continue into the election stage, and a final decision can be made without resort to formal proceedings of any kind. The regional director type of agreement is "the most frequently used method of informal adjustment of representation cases." [91] This fact is evidence of "public confidence in the overall competence and fairness of the Regional Directors and the desire of parties for an expeditious and informal procedure." [92]

Scope of NLRB Informal Adjudication

In recent years the NLRB has disposed of approximately 7,000 to 10,000 representation cases each year, a volume that would preclude extensive use of formal procedural techniques. The early use of informal procedure in this area by the Board is indicated in the NLRB case disposition table shown.

NLRB REPRESENTATION CASE DISPOSITION
1936–1950

Year (fiscal)	Cases closed before formal action No.	%	Cases closed after formal action No.	%
1936	90	88.2	12	11.8
1938	2,555	80.9	602	19.1
1940	1,966	73.1	724	26.9
1942	4,875	77.6	1,410	22.4
1944	4,353	66.9	2,154	33.1
1946	5,911	74.1	2,070	25.9
1948	5,613	82.3	1,204	17.7
1950	6,336	72.3	2,425	27.7

SOURCE: NLRB Annual Reports.

Both at the present time and in the past the Board has been able to settle informally, on an average, close to 75 per cent of all representation cases.

The accompanying table illustrates NLRB disposition in this area for a typical year at the present time.

Summary

The statutory requirement that the National Labor Relations Board determine the appropriate bargaining unit to represent designated groups of employees necessitates Board adjudication of a substantial number of application cases. Most of these applications are adjudicated informally. In many cases the petition to the Board for certification is dismissed because the unit does not represent a majority of the employees, or because the unit itself does not represent the particular skills of the employees. If a controversy exists, with respect to what unit should be certified, adjustment is effected through conference and through consent

NLRB REPRESENTATION CASE DISPOSITION, 1960

Method and stage of disposition	*No.*	*%*
Total number of cases closed	10,218	100.0
Consent election	2,834	27.7
Before notice of hearing	1,965	19.2
After notice of hearing, before hearing opened	750	7.3
After hearing opened, before Board decision	119	1.2
Stipulated election	1,898	18.6
Before notice of hearing	890	8.7
After notice of hearing, before hearing opened	712	7.0
After hearing opened, before Board decision	122	1.2
After postelection decision	174	1.7
Regional director-directed election	35	.3
Before notice of hearing	32	.3
After notice of hearing, before hearing opened	3	
Withdrawn	2,478	24.3
Before notice of hearing	1,506	14.7
After notice of hearing, before hearing opened	660	6.5
After hearing opened, before Board decision	160	1.6
After Board decision and direction of election	152	1.5
Dismissed	1,603	10.4
Before notice of hearing	616	6.0
After notice of hearing, before hearing opened	67	.7
After hearing opened, before Board decision	30	.3
By Board decision	350	3.4
Board ordered election	1,910	18.7

SOURCE: 1960 NLRB Annual Report, p. 189.

elections in most cases. Formal procedure in this adjudicative area, though it has more meaning than in those agencies previously examined, is clearly subordinate to the informal administrative process in scope and in importance.

CONCLUSION

The purpose of this chapter has been to point out, first, that within the administrative process an adjudicative area known as the application case area can be defined. This area is composed of those cases in which various types of applicants petition particular government agencies for permission to engage in activities which, by statute, cannot be undertaken without approval.

Within the scope of this book chapter iii has dealt specifically with the Securities and Exchange Commission, the Interstate Commerce Commission, the Federal Communications Commission, and the National Labor Relations Board. It has not included a vast area consisting of benefit applications, which will be described and analyzed at a later point, in terms of the Veterans Administration and the Social Security Administration, examples of what will be designated the "pure" adjudicative process. Further, this chapter has not included a discussion of the procedures of the Civil Aeronautics Board, for the application case area within the purview of that agency is characterized by legal requirements for formal procedure. The utilization of informal techniques by the CAB to overcome statutory barriers requiring formal hearings has been discussed fully in the preceding chapter concerning shortened procedure. Finally, the provisions of the Administrative Procedure Act have been discussed in general terms. But in many instances, because of such factors as the need for speed and the existence of administrative sanctions, provisions designed to protect individuals from arbitrary administrative action and provide judicial review have little meaning in reality.

From the examination of the agencies considered in this chapter, several significant points should be noted. First, in the process of adjudicating the various application cases within their jurisdiction, these agencies affect, to varying degrees, the nation as a whole, particular communities within the nation, and the individual applicants. In many instances the power of these agencies to adjudicate application cases becomes the power of life and death to particular corporate and individual enterprises. Because of this, the procedure used by such agencies in adjudicating applications, and the basis upon which their decisions are made, should conform to the democratic and constitutional postulates upon which our government is based.

Second, it has been demonstrated that in this application case area formal procedure generally is not used in the process of adjudication. Where it is used to any extent, it is clearly subordinate in scope and significance to informal procedure. The reasons for this situation are diverse. In general they center upon the need for dispatch, the desirability of lack of publicity, the

volume of cases, and the need to save expense. Informal procedure is expeditious, benefiting both the government and the
private interests involved.

Finally, the fact that clearly defined standards, such as those
procedural standards developed by the common law, are not followed by government agencies in the process of adjudication of
application cases essentially leaves each agency, and in many
cases each individual administrative official, free to develop independent procedural methods of an informal nature, varying with
the unique needs of the agency. Administrative discretion is not
only a fact of present governmental administration, but will
necessarily continue to expand as governmental regulation increases.

Chapter IV

COMPLAINT CASES

A significant proportion of the cases arising before administrative agencies requiring adjudication are concerned with securing compliance with statutes and administrative regulations. Such cases, which may be termed "complaint cases," develop either because one private party brings action against another for a violation of the law, or because the agency itself feels that corrective action must be taken, and hence registers a complaint against the party involved. In either case the complaint must be adjudicated by the agency. When the complaint is registered the agency may issue a formal complaint calling for a hearing, or it may settle the case informally. The latter may be accomplished through dismissal for lack of jurisdiction, because no reasonable grounds for the complaint exist, or through a process of informal adjustment. The purpose of this chapter is to examine the informal methods of disposition employed in the administrative process through reference to a selected number of agencies, and to note the quantitative and qualitative significance of such adjudication.

THE INTERNAL REVENUE SERVICE

Unquestionably the operation of the Internal Revenue Service exemplifies the most complex and vast use of informal procedure in the administrative process. The complexity stems from the nature of the subject matter with which the agency deals; the scope stems from the fact that most persons and corporations in the United States are directly affected by the collection of internal revenue.

The job of collection is rendered more difficult, and the need for informal and flexible adjudicative procedure is more acute, because of the fact that taxes are collected through a process of self-assessment. It is the responsibility of the taxpayer to assess himself or his business in accordance with the law. The essential

104

job of the Internal Revenue Service is to see to it that the individual taxpayer or corporation correctly assesses taxes owed the government and that it files a proper return.

The magnitude of IRS adjudication is indicated by the fact that in fiscal 1960 more than 94 million returns were filed, involving an amount in excess of $91 billion. Over 38 million refunds were made, in an amount over $5 billion. Theoretically, each of these returns presents a case for adjudication, for it is important to determine whether or not the taxpayer has conformed to legal requirements; in fact, however, the IRS is unable to audit all returns, and must rely upon sampling techniques to select initially returns for investigation and possible adjudication.

Because of the volume of cases involved (and it is proper to consider each return as a potential case, for nothing could be more controversial than the interpretation of internal revenue laws, where the IRS more frequently than not disagrees with private parties concerned) it would be clearly impossible for the IRS to conduct its business if formal procedure was utilized. Although the work of the IRS is primarily in the complaint case area, it does handle application cases in its supervision of the alcohol and tobacco industries. In this area alone, which is in the "pure administrative process," an area set apart by the extreme technical nature of the cases involved, the IRS adjudicated around 6,000 cases in fiscal 1960, issuing 3,000 permits and terminating around the same number. If cases involving approval of labels or exemption from requirements in this field are added to this total the number of cases involved is in excess of 40,000. Further, in line with supervision of these industries the service conducts over 30,000 investigations each year of establishments, and receives around 40,000 samples to determine conformity with the law.

Informal Conference Procedure

The IRS has emphasized informal adjudication throughout its history, and in 1952 a fundamental reorganization of the service was carried out which was designed to strengthen this aspect of their work through greater delegation of authority to field offices and standardization of procedure.

Historically, the service has attempted through various means to inform potential tax violators of deficiencies and gave them an opportunity to present their case before formal action was taken. The "thirty-day letter" was devised, which requested the opinion of the taxpayer with regard to proposed action. If the taxpayer disagreed with the validity of the action to be taken he would state the reasons for his disagreement, either through correspondence or conference. If the private party concerned failed to respond, this was taken as acceptance of proposed action, and an official statutory notice of deficiency was mailed. Even though such a deficiency notice was received, however, the taxpayer still had the opportunity to appeal a first-level adverse informal decison to an appellate division, where a new set of informal procedures were invoked to secure agreement.

Originally the appellate level informal conferences were conducted by the so-called Technical Staff, which was created in 1933 to settle informally as many cases scheduled to come before the Board of Tax Appeals (now the Tax Court) as possible. The Board itself was the only group within the service which utilized procedure approximating formal hearings. The Technical Staff was given jurisdiction over two categories of cases now handled by the Appellate Division. First, nondocketed cases (cases that had not been docketed formally with the Board of Tax Appeals). Second, docketed cases, scheduled for formal hearing before the Board of Tax Appeals. From initial informal conference levels taxpayers could appeal directly to the Board or to the initial appellate level, but it made little difference insofar as informal procedure was involved, for in either case the service attempted to secure informal agreement. If the taxpayer appealed first to the nondocketed stage, he would have to go through two series of informal conferences before his case could reach the Board of Tax Appeals, the first at the nondocketed stage, the second after his case was docketed. If, on the other hand, his initial appeal was to the docketed stage only, one informal attempt was made to settle the case before a hearing before the Board of Tax Appeals.

In 1952 the Technical Staff was renamed the Appellate Division and the Internal Revenue Service was reorganized to strengthen the effectiveness of informal procedure. It was also at this time that all appointive offices in the service save that of the Commissioner were abolished. The organizational changes involving informal settlement procedure that were effected were as follows:

(1) the transfer of the 12-district, nationwide Appellate Staff force, including personnel of the Chief Counsel engaged in appellate work, into the Appellate Divisions of district commissioners' offices;

(2) the abolition of the 39 internal revenue agents conference sections and the merger of their personnel and workload into the Appellate Divisions;

(3) the complete redelegation of final settlement authority to the associate head of each Appellate Division and the limited redelegation of final settlement authority to the assistant heads and special assistants to the head of each Appellate Division; and

(4) the establishment of the informal conference procedure to provide an appeal opportunity in each of the 64 district directors' offices prior to the preparation of the examiner's final report and with no requirement for a written protest by the taxpayer.[1]

This reorganization strengthened the effectiveness of informal procedure used by the service by delegating final settlement authority to field divisions and by integrating the informal conference procedure at the initial level.

The objectives of the new initial informal conference procedure are described by the IRS as follows:

The objective of the informal conference procedure is to give taxpayers greater opportunity to reach an early agreement with respect to disputed items arising from examination made by internal revenue agents through the use of an informal procedure by means of which such issues may be resolved prior to the preparation of the . . . agent's final report. Through this means, the disposition of disputed cases will be brought closer to the taxpayer, improved coördination and supervision of the activities of field examiners will be achieved, and the closing of cases by agreement without the necessity of the taxpayer filing a formal protest will be increased.[2]

At this initial level, "the original examination of income, profits, estate, gift, excise and employment tax liability will be the primary function of internal revenue agents assigned as examining officers in the audit branch of the office of each Director of Internal Revenue. Such . . . agents will be organized in groups, each of which will be under the immediate supervision of a group chief, designated by the Director. The present groups will be reduced in size and additional groups created so that, in addition to his general supervisory responsibilities, each group chief may act in the capacity of conferee. . . ." [3] If it is found that a potential tax deficiency exists in any particular return, and if a field audit is felt to be necessary, the audit is conducted by an internal revenue agent assigned as examining officer. After mathematical verification of returns a selection of questionable specimens is made. The basic selection principle is to determine which returns indicate the greatest deficiency or overassessment. Because of the number of returns involved, mathematical verification pertains only to individual returns, and even at that it is somewhat limited in scope. In fiscal 1960, for example, only 50 million, out of approximately 60 million individual returns, were mathematically verified. Of this number approximately 2 million were found in error, about two-thirds in favor of the individuals and one-third in favor of the government. Revenue increase to the government, as a result of such determinations, amounted to $112 million, with $48 million being returned to individuals.

Revenue Service audits of returns are conducted through correspondence at the office level, and through personal contact with the taxpayer in the field. Relative to the area of mathematical certification the audit is adjudicative in nature, requiring judgment on the part of the agent in the exercise of what is in fact discretionary power, although he operates within the framework of regulations, most of which have been established by the service itself within a very broad congressional delegation of power. As indicated above, the purpose of auditing as it is now conducted is to gain revenue for the government through the "correction" of returns, mostly by corporations, containing errors in their interpretation of revenue laws. Needless to say, the IRS would not put this statement in such positive terms; however, the fact remains that they do not want to waste the time of the limited number of people they employ in an intensive auditing of returns that contain little if any possibility of a substantial net gain to the government. An idea of the quantitative scope of IRS audits is illustrated by the fact that in fiscal 1960, 3 million returns were examined in total, of which 2 million comprised office audits and around 1 million were field examinations. This indicates that less than 5 per cent of the total number of returns filed with the service are examined through the auditing procedure. Nevertheless, to illustrate the validity of the motive of the service in conducting such audits, in fiscal 1960, $1.8 billion was collected in additional tax plus interest, almost all of which was obtained from corporations.

With respect to those returns selected for audit, at the conclusion of the initial examination the internal revenue agent discusses his findings with the individual or corporate taxpayer, affording him an opportunity to settle through the execution of an agreement, which essentially waives the individual's rights to further judicial proceedings within or without the administrative process. However, if the taxpayer does not wish to enter into agreement as a result of this "discussion" with the agent, he is informed of his right of appeal and is furnished with a statement apprising him of the proposed adjustment which will provide the basis of subsequent informal proceedings. This latter technique is a form of informal notice. In the words of IRS regulations the explanations of adjustments "will be brief but will adequately identify each issue, set forth the reasons for the proposed adjustments, and contain sufficient information for the Conference Coördinator to properly evaluate and assign the conference, and to permit the conferee, taxpayer, and tax practitioner to understand the issues." [4]

Initial appeal is taken to the district office, where a Conference Coördinator is in charge of arranging conferences and selecting conferees as well as implementing standards to be followed in the conference process. The Coördinator is instructed to take special care in the designation of the conferee, who should be the best qualified to dispose effectively and fairly of the proceeding under review. Technical *expertise* is taken into account in difficult cases, and certain judicial standards of fairness are followed even at this level.

The Revenue Service has defined procedural and substantive standards of conduct for the district office conference:

> In the conduct of informal conferences it will be the duty of the . . . conferee to conduct the conference in accordance with the objectives of the informal conference procedure and to——
>
> (a) Provide the taxpayer a fair and courteous hearing at which he may present his statement of the facts and his view on the issues;
>
> (b) Make certain that all pertinent facts are included in the record and are considered in arriving at the proposed recommendation;
>
> (c) Make certain that the appropriate provisions of the Internal Revenue Code are applied in arriving at the proposed recommendation;
>
> (d) Make certain that the proposed recommendation is in accord with Bureau [IRS] interpretations as expressed in regulations and rulings; and
>
> (e) Explain fully to the taxpayer the conclusion reached and the reasons therefor.[5]

Such standards are designed to guarantee the taxpayer a fair hearing in accordance with the law. All of the aspects of a particular case are to be considered and are to be included in a record. Needless to say, the success of such procedure depends entirely upon the conduct of the conferee, although further review is easily obtained on an informal basis.

After the initial appellate conference in the district office the taxpayer is notified in a "30-day letter" of proposed action by the service. Once again, if he agrees he may sign a waiver of his rights of further appeal; however, if he fails to agree he may obtain an informal hearing in the Appellate Division, where standards and procedures similar to those noted with respect to the preappellate level are followed, and the stages formerly followed by the Technical Staff (nondocketed and docketed) are in effect.

In summary, the IRS now has a highly structured informal adjudicative network designed to secure settlement of most revenue cases before resort to the formal process represented by the Tax Court. Informal conferences now take place at three levels:

(1) the conference between the examining officer and the taxpayer at the initial audit stage; (2) if agreement is not reached at the audit stage informal conferences take place at the district office level; (3) final informal appeal may be taken to the Appellate Division, in which several opportunities for conferences are presented. The IRS leaves no stone unturned in its attempt to effect informal disposition of tax cases.

Evaluation of Informal Conference Procedure

As will be indicated below, the success of IRS informal adjudication in effecting settlement is outstanding; however, certain criticisms have been advanced regarding the system followed. In 1955 an advisory group to the Joint Congressional Committee on Internal Revenue Taxation prepared a report criticizing the new procedures of the IRS in informal adjudication. This group felt that

> under the old system the taxpayer had every conference opportunity that is afforded by the new; and, in addition, a right to a conference before the conference section of the agent in charge. This conference section played no part in setting up the tax to which the taxpayer was objecting. It functioned under its own chief conferee and was administratively free from the group chiefs and the review section. The conference section performed a very useful function not only from a public-relations standpoint but also in reducing the pre-90-day workload of the Appellate Division and stabilizing the settlement activities of the agent's office.[6]

It is true that under the informal procedure used by the Revenue Service before its reorganization there was a greater separation between the attempts to adjust a case informally at the audit stage and at the first appeal stage, for the personnel before whom informal appeal could be taken in the office of the agent-in-charge were not directly connected with those conducting the original audit. Also, under the former system, a series of conferences might take place in the office of the agent-in-charge, resulting in what can properly be described as an interoffice informal appeal system, although essentially the same thing operates today within the district office of the IRS, from which appeal may be taken to the Appellate Division.

Apart from criticisms pertaining to an insufficient lack of separation of functions within the informal adjudicative procedure of the IRS, the advisory group voiced a traditional legal anxiety when it noted that "the absence of a [an adequate] record showing the issues and conclusion reached in the settlement at the pre-appellate level may operate unfairly both with respect to the taxpayer and the Government. Many practitioners have indicated that under the informal procedure some issues are entirely overlooked by the agents in the initial examinations. In fact, some practitioners have disclosed that cases with controversial issues have been settled in a few hours on minor issues, the large major issues being entirely overlooked. This, of course, is a real danger to the Government revenues." [7] The facts do not seem to bear this criticism out, as the agents seem able to increase substantially government revenues by means of a careful selection and auditing of returns. More frequently than not, it is their excessive diligence, rather than their apathy, that is criticized.

Turning to a statistical evaluation of the informal procedure employed by the IRS a number of indicators illustrate the significance of such adjudication. First, it is important to note that a substantial degree of final adjudication results from the mere designation of an income tax return deficient because of the failure of respondents to challenge the decision by the Revenue Service. The accompanying table contains the number of in-

IRS PROTESTED CASES

Calendar year	Individual and fiduciary income tax returns involving deficiencies			Corporation income returns involving deficiencies		
	Total No.	Protested	%	Total No.	Protested	%
1952	259,766	17,996	6.9	53,235	5,109	9.6
1953	324,398	7,260	2.2	45,229	1,958	4.3
1954	554,301	7,730	1.4	52,256	2,004	3.8

SOURCE: *U.S. Cong., Joint ,Committee on Internal Revenue Taxation, The Internal Revenue Service, Its Reorganization and Administration* (Wash., 1955), p. 8.

dividual and fiduciary income tax returns involving deficiencies for the period 1952–1954 (figures are unavailable for subsequent years) and the number of such returns protested. The sharp drop in the number of protested cases after 1952 came because the term "protested return" was redefined to mean only those protests coming *after* failure to reach initial agreement in the pre-appellate conference stage in the district offices. It is evident that approximately 85 per cent of the cases involving deficiencies are settled informally through the acceptance on the part of the taxpayer of the initial decision of the Revenue Service.[8] Under the new informal conference procedure settlement is reached in the preappellate stage in approximately 95 per cent of the cases involving deficiencies. This can easily be seen in the 1953 and 1954 figures, where those cases protested represent pre-appellate failure to reach agreement and hence are taken on appeal to the Appellate Division. Taking individual and fiduciary returns in 1954 separately from corporation returns, 98.6 per cent were settled informally at the preappellate level.

Through interpolation from the table, the following additional conclusions may be stated: (1) informal conference procedure at the preappellate stage settles approximately 80 per cent of the individual and fiduciary income tax return cases involving deficiencies *contested* by the taxpayer; and (2) approximately 60 per cent of contested corporation income tax return cases involving deficiencies are settled at this stage informally.[9]

Turning to an evaluation of present Appellate Division informal adjudication, by fiscal 1960 its workload had increased substantially to a point where it was handling over 23,000 pending and new protested cases in the nondocketed category, due to the increasing number of returns and larger volume at the preappellate stage. Out of this volume of cases handled, less than 3,000 were finally petitioned to the Tax Court from the decision of the division during the year. In the docketed category approximately 7,000 cases, new and pending, were adjudicated during fiscal 1960, about 6,000 being settled informally, with almost 1,000 being tried before the Court on the merits. Thus about 4 per cent of those cases handled by the Appellate Division reach the Tax Court, and less than 1 per cent of the total number of cases handled by the Revenue Service at both the appellate and preappellate stages reach the formal process of the Tax Court.

Not only is informal adjudication by the Appellate Division quantitatively and qualitatively more important than that performed by the Tax Court; it also exceeds in importance in these respects those cases involving taxpayer's suits in the Federal District Courts and the Court of Claims. Taxpayers have recourse to either of the courts for redress of grievances. In fiscal 1960 these courts combined disposed of 1,000 cases involving around $146 million, which compares with 30,000 cases handled by the Appellate Division involving disputed amounts in excess of $1.25 billion.

Informal Interpretative Advice

The Revenue Service gives a great deal of informal interpretative advice to taxpayers, both general and specific. This activity is not adjudication in the strict sense; however, it affects the adjudicative area by rendering decisions in advance which prevent the development of a contested case. In many instances such decision-making should properly be considered similar to but one step removed from informal adjudication. In general terms the IRS prepares many types of books, pamphlets, and circulars regarding particular tax areas. The most famous booklet is entitled *Your Federal Income Tax;* other booklets are directed at farmers, small businessmen, and other groups which may have unique problems with regard to revenue collection. Booklets are directed at special problems as well as at particular groups.

In addition to this general advice, the IRS gives technical advice to specific requests for such. During fiscal 1960 the service processed over 33,000 requests from taxpayers and over 3,000 from field offices concerning particular tax problems. Further, in this same year the service received over 10 million requests for aid from individual taxpayers in the preparation of their returns. Of this number over 5 million were assisted by telephone, more than 4 million in groups to which revenue agents were assigned for advice, and almost half a million were assisted individually. In this way the service is able to shape the interpretation of the tax laws by individual taxpayers and prevent the development of a volume of cases that could not be handled within the existing administrative framework of the agency.

Summary

It is evident that quantitatively and qualitatively the job of adjudicating cases arising within the jurisdiction of the Internal Revenue Service is one of the greatest in the administrative branch of the government. Each year, over 90 million returns must be processed involving tens of billions of dollars.

Of all cases involving adjudicative decisions 99 per cent are settled informally by the IRS. The relative lack of importance of the Tax Court within the administrative branch, and the Federal District Courts and the Court of Claims on the outside, has been demonstrated. Formal procedure is used before these courts.

The Revenue Service has built an elaborate procedural network characterized by informal procedure and designed to settle all tax cases that are in any way amenable to informal settlement. A series of informal conferences takes place at both the pre-appellate and appellate stage, with the taxpayer being afforded the opportunity to participate in at least four such conferences before taking his case to the Tax Court.

It is important to note that *standards*, both procedural and substantive, have been defined by the IRS with respect to the informal settlement of cases, both at the initial and at the appellate levels. These standards are designed to provide the taxpayer with a fair hearing in accordance with the law, and they provide some basis upon which a fair decision may be rendered. Needless to say, the success of such criteria depends upon the caliber of the personnel charged with implementing them. In this area, as in most areas of informal adjudication, limitation of administrative action must be internal, for no effective external means of control exist. Because of the importance of IRS adjudication, both to the government and to those persons or corporations specifically affected, the problem of administrative responsibility is particularly acute in this area.

It is evident from an examination of the operations of the IRS that formalization of the adjudicative process within the agency would place an impossible burden upon governmental machinery for tax collection and would also prevent administrative justice from being realized with respect to the individuals concerned in tax cases, for the burdens of formal procedure would defeat the purposes of adjudication in terms of time and expense. The predominant role of informal procedure is necessitated by: (1) the volume of cases coming before the IRS and the consequent need for speed, to aid effective governmental action and to protect the parties concerned from prolonged litigation; (2) the expense inherent in formal proceedings, which automatically defeats the purposes of fair adjudication in many instances.

Finally, it must be pointed out that the Internal Revenue Service affects persons in their capacity as individuals more than is the case with many other agencies engaged in administrative adjudication. In cases involving individuals as opposed to those where corporations or other economically powerful groups are parties, agency discretion is increased because of the lack of balanced resources between the agency and the parties coming within its jurisdiction. As a general rule, individuals do not have the time, the money, or the understanding necessary to take their case to the formal administrative process, let alone to the courts; therefore, they must adjust their case informally at the initial stage without the benefit of formal procedure and a decision on the record. In such instances, the possibility of further appeal is eliminated.

THE FEDERAL TRADE COMMISSION

The adjudicative activities of the FTC fall primarily within the category of complaint cases. The Commission is charged with maintaining free competition through the prevention of practices tending to a restraint of trade, and, in addition, it regulates deceptive practices directed by various types of business interests against the public. In both areas, the Commission affects substantial economic interests, regulating their ability to expand through acquisition, and their techniques of selling and representing products to the public. And in both types of cases complaints are made in the name of the Commission against a private party, although any interested private or public party may make the initial complaint to the FTC. The names of complainants are held in confidence as a matter of policy, for divulging names might bring economic retaliation. Indeed this was one of the indiscretions of President Eisenhower's assistant Sherman Adams, who secured from the chairman of the FTC the name of a complainant against the notorious Bernard Goldfine and subsequently divulged it to Goldfine.[10]

The Commission utilizes several types of informal settlement techniques, including stipulations, consent orders, and trade practice conferences. The latter are designed to formulate in advance trade regulations which have the effect in some instances of settling pending cases through acceptance by the parties involved of the decisions of the conference.

In the first years of the Commission's operation informal disposition was a vital part of its adjudicative procedure. This was expressed in an early report.

> Before the issuance of a formal complaint the Commission notifies the party complained of that the charges have been made, giving a statement thereof, and also informing such party that it is not the policy of the Commission to institute formal proceedings thereon without first making a full investigation of the facts, stating to such party that it will have an opportunity to be heard in reference thereto and to explain or deny the alleged violation of law.
>
> This policy has been very successful not only in avoiding ill-founded prosecution but also because in a number of notable instances, although there appeared to be a violation of law, still the party complained against agreed to cease and desist therefrom and in such cases the Commission thus far has not instituted a proceeding, but has dismissed the case by a conference ruling. . . .
>
> Thus far where the parties complained of have ceased and desisted from the violations charged, it has been considered that the public interests have been as well served as they would have been if a formal proceeding were instituted and the Commission and the respondent required to indulge in expensive and prolonged litigation.[11]

From the very beginning, the FTC has adopted procedure which it has felt best furthers the public interest in accordance with the law. The primary aim of the Commission being to effect compliance with the regulations governing the monopolistic and deceptive practice fields, it has felt in many instances that informal procedure accomplishes this purpose without undue delay and expense, which if excessive might violate the public interest.

As indicated above, during the early years of operation, agreement to cease and desist was sufficient cause for dismissal of a Commission action against a respondent. During this period the term "conference ruling" referred to a decision resulting from an informal conference between the parties involved and the Commission. These rulings were published and used to some extent as precedent, which indicated the desire of the Commission to form some substantive guidelines for the informal adjudicative area.

As the FTC developed, its informal procedure began to take more definite form. The stipulation, which is no longer used (as of June, 1962), was first employed in 1925. In 1926 the Commission noted that before a formal complaint was issued several stages had to be passed. First, "if the material examined is not within the jurisdiction of the Commission or is without merit, or if the matter is satisfactorily disposed of by conference or correspondence, the file is closed as an 'undocketed application.'" [12] If this initial procedure did not result in settlement the application was docketed, but informal agreement was still attempted in the form of a stipulation. In a stipulation, as opposed to the earlier conference ruling, the facts stated could be used by the Commission against the respondent in future proceedings. On the other hand, no illegal action needed to be admitted by the respondent. Unfair methods of competition or deceptive practices were generally alleged, but not proven or admitted. The Commission felt that the stipulation procedure would be as effective in securing informal agreement as the conference ruling, but would not hamper the Commission if further action was required. The fact that conference rulings were frequently violated provided further reason for stipulated agreements.

The FTC is not required by law to hold formal hearings. Section 5(b) of the Federal Trade Commission Act provides that

Whenever the Commission shall have reason to believe that any such person, partnership, or corporation has been or is using any unfair method of competition or deceptive act or practice in commerce, and if it shall appear to the

> Commission that a proceeding by it in respect thereof would
> be to the interest of the public . . . it shall issue . . . a
> complaint stating its charges in that respect and containing
> a notice of hearing. . . .[13]

In line with this provision, a formal proceeding is necessary only
where the Commission feels it would be in the public interest.
Although the stipulation procedure is not directly mentioned by
law, it is nevertheless within the spirit of the law.

In 1946 the FTC created a separate Division of Stipulations,
to expedite and coördinate settlement through this device. In the
same year the stipulation procedure was made more flexible to
permit respondents to present their side of the case to FTC
representatives. Less emphasis was given by the Commission to
procedure whereby respondents were encouraged to stipulate on
the government's terms or else face formal complaint proceedings. The Division of Stipulations acted only when the Bureau
of Investigation found practices which it believed were violative
of law. In this way informal investigation, with a view to possible prosecution if informal settlement should fail, was func-
tionally separated from informal adjudication.

Admissive Answers and Administrative Consent Settlement

If the FTC is unable to effect informal settlement of a complaint, recourse is necessarily made to the formal administrative
process. This adjudicative area is characterized, if the party
complained against so desires, by formal hearings which may
or may not result in Commission issuance of a formal cease and
desist order. Informal settlement procedures are still operative
at this level, however, because of Commission rules providing
for the filing of an admissive answer on the part of the respondent
and providing for consent settlement.

With regard to the procedure for the filing of an admissive
answer, the Rules of Practice of the FTC provided for the first
time in 1927 that, after the Commission had served upon the
respondent a statement of charges and notice of hearing, the
hearing might be waived on the following basis:

> In case respondent desires to waive hearing on the charges
> set forth in the complaint and not to contest the proceeding,
> the *answer* may consist of a statement that respondent re-

frains from contesting the proceeding or that respondent consents that the Commission may make, enter, and serve upon respondent an order to cease and desist from the *violations of the law* alleged in the complaint, or that respondent admits all the allegations of the complaint to be true. Any such answer shall be deemed to be an admission of all the allegations of the complaint and to authorize the Commission to find such allegations to be true.[14]

In 1938 this provision was changed to enable respondents to challenge, in writing or orally, the alleged illegality derived by the Commission from the facts.

The extent to which the FTC has settled formal complaint cases without holding formal hearings, or granting oral argument, is impressive. The records of the Commission indicate that from 1915 through fiscal year 1952 there were 4,343 formal cease and desist orders issued. Of this number, 2,764 were contested and 1,579 were admissive.[15] Thus 29 per cent of the formal complaint cases were settled by admissive answers without contest.

Although the admissive answer procedure was an admitted success, it was felt that an even more flexible informal device might settle a greater percentage of cases scheduled for formal proceedings. With regard to the admissive answer procedure the Commission noted in 1951 that "reluctance of respondents to admit having engaged in unlawful practices has in the past resulted in long and expensive litigation in some instances where, except for the necessity of such admissions, the proceeding might have been settled without trial." [16] Because of this need for greater flexibility, the Commission adopted a new consent order procedure in 1951, which was first put into practice in 1952. In essence this is a more formal type of stipulation, negotiated after initial informal settlement has failed. The important difference in this type of consent order and the former admissive answer is the fact that respondents are not necessarily required to admit a legal violation. The success of this new form of consent order is indicated by the fact that in 1952 only 10 per cent of the total number of cease-and-desist orders were settled in this manner, whereas in fiscal 1960 out of 346 cease-and-desist orders 285 were fully settled by consent and 8 partially settled in this way; thus at the present time over 80 per cent of these formal order cases are settled by consent.

In July, 1961, the FTC adopted new procedural rules regarding consent settlements that were designed to speed up its enforcement procedure through even greater informality. Under the new rules, the FTC will inform respondents of violations in advance of the issuance of a cease-and-desist order, and give the party ten days to decide if it wishes to negotiate a settlement. If the respondent refuses to settle informally, the Commission will file formal charges which cannot thereafter be settled by consent. Further, the Commission delegated greater power to its trial examiners by requiring at least two Commission votes on appeal before review will be undertaken of the examiners' decision. These and other procedures were adopted, emphasizing, among other things, the importance of informal procedure and delegation of power to the work of the FTC. The stipulation has now been discontinued. It is the hope of the Commission that its new consent order procedure will provide enough opportunity for informal settlement so that the former stipulation procedure will not be missed.

Other Methods of Informal Settlement

above, the FTC employs (1) trade practice conferences and (2) initial informal conferences and correspondence to settle cases.

Trade practice conferences take place between the FTC and industry representatives in order to: (1) define the legality of certain trade practices; (2) afford the industry groups concerned the opportunity to state their views concerning what they consider to be desirable practices. These conferences have a preventive function, decreasing the potential future Commission work load in adjudication, and they provide as well for industry participation in the rule-making process. In many instances informal conferences precede and follow trade practice conferences. The FTC seeks to secure written acceptance with regard to the rules formulated from trade conferences. After these rules have been agreed upon the Commission examines all charges of legal violations pertaining to industry members, provided a formal complaint has not been issued. Where pending charges are covered by conference rules, the FTC may informally close the case, if it has reason to believe that the party involved will comply with the rules. Even a formal complaint may be suspended through acceptance on the part of a respondent of such rules. After all, a successful trade practice conference is a manifestation of consent between the Commission and the particular members of the industry that subscribe to the conference rules, and the existence of such consent enables the Commission to adjudicate pending cases on the basis of conference decisions, for to the extent that this consent is operative compliance is assured. In this manner, through the trade practice conference procedure informal rule-making results in informal adjudication.

The second significant stage in which informal settlement takes place is at the initial complaint level, before any attempt is made to stipulate. In fiscal 1960 the FTC received close to 6,000 complaint letters; however, only 500 complaints were issued, which indicates a significant informal disposition at the precomplaint stage. At this stage the Commission may accept affidavits of discontinuance or even voluntary abandonment of the questioned practices as adequate to dispose of the case informally in the public interest. The Commission has noted that in many cases the mere initiation of an investigation causes cessation of unlawful practices. Further, investigation of a complaint may show insufficient grounds for further Commission action. Regardless of the reasons, which are varied, a large number of cases are settled informally at this level.

Statistical Summary

It is possible to view the adjudicative activities of the FTC discussed above in terms of the table shown herewith, which covers the years 1915–1954.

It is evident from the table that during this period only 20 per cent of the applications reached the formal complaint stage; 30 per cent were settled by stipulation to cease and desist from practices in violation of law; and almost 50 per cent were dismissed or closed without further proceedings. Many of the cases settled in the latter category represent informal adjudication.

APPLICATIONS FOR COMPLAINTS—CUMULATIVE SUMMARY
1915–1954

1. Applications docketed	25,909
2. Total for disposition after changes	
in previous action	26,318
3. Action:	
To complaints	5,660
Settled by stipulation to cease and desist	7,479
Settled by acceptance of TPC rules	97
Consolidated with other proceedings	213
Dismissed	3,880
Closed without further proceedings	6,278
Dismissed or closed	1,545
Total Disposition	25,152

SOURCE: FTC Annual Reports and letter to the author. Figures after 1954, in these categories, are unavailable because of a revised reporting system.

Within this category are contained cases dismissed for lack of merit and cases closed without further proceedings because of acceptance of assurance of discontinuance, business or practices discontinued, and the like. In many such instances administrative judgment must be exercised; thus the large number of cases in this category suggests the significance of highly informal procedure, relative even to informal stipulation procedure. In recent years, before discontinuance of the stipulation, the proportion of cases settled through the various procedures employed has been roughly the same as that represented in the table. This may be seen from the fiscal 1960 work load of the Commission, when it received 5,930 applications for complaint, and issued only 503 complaints of which 112 were stipulated agreements.

Summary

In summary, the adjudicative methods of the FTC in the informal sphere are composed of a variety of devices. The conference ruling, an informal opinion of the Commission with respect to the settlement of a complaint case on the basis of the cessation of the questionable activity by the respondent, was utilized extensively at first. This practice eventually evolved into the stipulation which has now been replaced by an informal consent order procedure. Through the stipulation informal settlement was effected when the respondent, agreeing to a stipulated set of facts which could be used in a later proceeding against him, but not admitting illegal action, ceased and desisted from the activity under question.

Before the stipulation (now the consent order) stage is reached, however, there is statistical evidence to suggest that extensive informal settlement procedures are used in the investigative stage of a complaint. A case may be settled by correspondence or conference, either at the pre-docketed or at the docketed level. This initial informal stage has become increasingly important in recent years.

The FTC may also dispose of a case informally on the basis of the respondent's acceptance of pertinent trade practice conference rules. Such rules are formulated through informal procedures consisting primarily of conferences between the Commission's staff and industry representatives. However, less than 3 per cent of the complaint cases are settled in this manner.

A further significant area in which the Commission's staff effects informal settlement is in the administration of the Wool, Fur, and Flammable Fabrics acts, which require proper labeling. In this area the Commission now administers an additional Textile Fiber Products Identification Act (1958). The Commission handles from 7,000 to 10,000 cases informally in this area each year.

Finally, even after a complaint case reaches the formal adjudicative stage informal settlement may be effected through the admissive answer and consent order procedures. The latter technique was developed to permit informal settlement without necessitating an admission of illegal action on the part of the respondent. The greatly increased use of the consent order, relative to that of the admissive answer, in bringing about settlement suggests the efficacy of this procedure.

In general, not taking into account the Wool, Fur, Flammable Fabrics and Textile acts, today less than 20 per cent of the complaint cases arising under the jurisdiction of the FTC in the docketed category reach the formal stage of adjudication. The firm dominance of FTC adjudication by informal procedural methods is evident.

THE NATIONAL LABOR RELATIONS BOARD

Section 8 of the National Labor Relations Act of 1935 defines standards of conduct for employers in order to aid employees to organize and bargain collectively through representatives of their own choosing. Under section 8: (1) employers cannot interfere with the right of employees to organize; (2) employers cannot dominate a labor organization; (3) they cannot discriminate against an employee of a union with regard to conditions of employment, and so forth; (4) they cannot fire or discriminate against an employee who has filed charges and/or testified against an employer; (5) employers must bargain collectively with union representatives.

Under the Taft-Hartley Act standards of conduct were extended to unions. The act provides that labor organizations cannot: (1) coerce employees with regard to their rights to organize, or coerce an employer in the choice of his bargaining agent; (2) cause, or coerce, an employer to discriminate against an employee for his failure to join a union, except under an authorized union-shop agreement; (3) fail to bargain collectively with an employer; (4) utilize the strike as a weapon for certain defined illegal actions, such as forcing an employer to accept a non-certified labor union; (5) institute excessive initiation fees, as determined by the Board; (6) extort employers.

Complaint cases are initiated by those coming within the jurisdiction of the Board, and are based upon the statutory provisions mentioned above. The Board has little direct formal enforcement power, and must rely upon the United States Courts of Appeal to enforce formal orders, and upon District Courts for injunctive relief against unfair labor practices. It can reinstate employees with or without pay, the only monetary deterrent it possesses. Regardless of this situation the Board has been able to employ informal procedure effectively to settle complaint cases. This procedure is provided for in the regulations of the Board, which encourage its use for settlement purposes both before and after formal complaint proceedings materialize. In terms of these procedural rules parties are to be given every opportunity to settle their case informally, regardless of the stage of the proceedings before the Board.

The National Labor Relations Act of 1947, moreover, provides for private informal adjustment of jurisdictional disputes by stating that:

> Whenever it is charged that any person has engaged in an unfair labor practice within the meaning of paragraph (4) (D) of section 8(b), the Board is empowered and directed to hear and determine the dispute . . . unless, within ten days after notice that such charge has been filed, the parties to such dispute submit to the Board satisfactory evidence that they have adjusted, or agreed upon methods for the voluntary adjustment of, the dispute. Upon compliance by the parties to the dispute with the decision of the Board or upon such voluntary adjustment of the dispute, such charge shall be dismissed.[17]

Scope and Techniques of Informal Adjudication

The key to NLRB informal adjudication is the field examiner, with whom parties in dispute come into contact, and who more frequently than not disposes of the case informally through conference. The informal conference in the field is much like an arbitration, conducted with varying degrees of formality with respect to procedure in accordance with the needs of the case and the demands of the parties. Records may or may not be kept; a complaint may or may not issue. In some cases the examiner will request the complainant to withdraw his charges. In others complaints will be dismissed for lack of supporting evidence. Generally the procedure employed at this level is highly flexible, and although it is theoretically only the initial stage of adjudication final decisions are made in the vast majority of cases.

As is true with most regulatory agencies, the NLRB has employed informal procedure extensively from the very beginning. Even in the early, heated, days of the Board's operation approximately 43 per cent of the charges filed were withdrawn or dismissed after initial informal adjudication.[18] The present effectiveness of initial informal settlement is indicated by the fact that in fiscal 1960 the field staff settled 10,309 unfair labor practice cases: 14 per cent were adjusted by various forms of settlement;

39 per cent were administratively dismissed after investigation; 47 per cent were withdrawn. In the latter category the Board has stated that in many of these cases "the withdrawals actually reflected settlement of the matter at issue between the parties." [19] In other words, the withdrawn cases reflected informal disposition.

From a general viewpoint the various stages of informal adjudication and their significance may be observed in the table show-

UNFAIR LABOR PRACTICE CASES CLOSED, FISCAL YEAR 1960

Stage of disposition	No. of cases	% closed
1. Before issuance of complaint	10,309	86.5
2. After issuance of complaint, before opening of hearing	767	6.4
3. After hearing opened, before issuance of intermediate report	185	1.6
4. After intermediate report, before issuance of Board decision	116	1.0
5. After Board order adopting intermediate report in absence of exceptions	117	1.0
6. After Board decisions, before court decree	275	2.3
7. After circuit court decree, before Supreme Court action	135	1.1
8. After Supreme Court action	20	.1
Total	11,924	100.0

SOURCE: 1960 NLRB Annual Report, p. 188.

ing the disposition of unfair labor practice cases in fiscal 1960. Although 86.5 per cent are closed informally before issuance of a complaint, over 92 per cent are closed before the opening of hearings. The adversary process, insofar as it is employed at all, affects less than 8 per cent of the cases coming before the NLRB. Over the years, the percentage of cases settled informally has varied, but on the average about 88 per cent have been disposed of in this manner. The highest percentage of cases reaching the formal administrative process in the history of the operation of the NLRB is 16.6, which occurred in 1954.[20]

Evaluation

The NLRB, like the other regulatory bodies, has policy as well as adjudicative responsibilities. The two are, of course, closely connected, and to a considerable degree the Board must utilize informal procedure in its adjudicative process if it is not to defeat the implementation of many important substantive policy standards. Voluntary compliance avoids time and expense, as well as ill feelings between labor and management. This latter consideration is particularly important, for the primary purpose of the National Labor Relations Act is to prevent unfair labor practices by employers, and with the amendments of 1947, prohibitions have been extended to unions as well. Formal adversary proceedings might create tension between labor and management that would hinder the development of friendly relationships. Without a voluntary agreement between these parties to abide by unfair labor practice standards the entire system would break down once the NLRB's surveillance relaxed.

In its first Annual Report the Board noted:

> There is no way of avoiding a certain amount of delay in the formal procedure before the Board and the courts required under the Act. . . . Therefore the ability of the regional offices to secure settlements before formal action became necessary has meant the rapid removal from the area of possible industrial conflict certain disputes which by their nature are likely to lead to economic strife. The benefits of such settlements have accrued to the employers and employees directly involved, as well as to the general public.[21]

The courts as well as the practitioners have recognized the vitality of the informal process used by the NLRB. In a series of cases the courts have upheld the Board when it has been necessary for it to resort to the formal process to enforce agreements made at the informal stage.[22] On judicial review the courts have been very reluctant to interfere with any Board procedure which facilitates inexpensive and expeditious procedure. This is particularly interesting in view of the fact that such procedure does not in the strict sense meet the requirements of due process, where notice and hearing is theoretically a minimum standard, and where findings of fact and other criteria are generally necessary.

The problem of administrative responsibility is not as acute in the area of adjudication of unfair labor practice cases as it is in many other places in the administrative process. Enforcement proceedings must be taken to the courts, and although deference is given there to administrative *expertise*, private parties nevertheless have a potential opportunity for a full-fledged formal hearing. In addition, the NLRB is not able to invoke administrative sanctions automatically through the initiation of formal action as is the case with such agencies as the SEC. The only penalty necessarily involved in taking a case to the formal hearing stage is time and expense. Such administrative sanctions as adverse publicity, for example, would not force private parties to settle informally. Further, the NLRB usually deals with economic groups possessing powerful financial and political resources in enforcement proceedings. This is in sharp contrast to any agency such as the Internal Revenue Service, which, in addition to corporations, deals to a considerable extent with individuals with insignificant financial and political power. The groups with which the NLRB deals are not particularly vulnerable; they are easily able to take a case to the formal administrative process and from there to the courts if necessary. This, of course, lessens the possibility of coercion at the informal adjudicative level. The net result of these factors is that the success of the informal settlement procedures used by the NLRB can as a general rule be attributed to the free consent of the private parties involved.

THE INTERSTATE COMMERCE COMMISSION

The Interstate Commerce Commission has established an elabo rate system to effect the informal settlement of complaint cases arising within their jurisdiction. Sections have been established to deal with informal cases in the areas of: (1) carrier-shipper relations involving rates; (2) service complaints; (3) demurrage disputes; (4) disputes relating to the operation of motor carriers.

Generally, complaint letters may be of an informal nature and will be accepted by the Commission. The present Rules of Practice provide that if possible informal settlement will be reached through correspondence to prevent the filing of a formal complaint.[23] Informal proceedings are without prejudice to the complainant's right to file a formal complaint. Of course, as discussed in chapter ii, various types of informal techniques are employed in the formal stage of adjudication to bring about expeditious and inexpensive settlement, even though upon the filing of a formal complaint informal proceedings are theoretically discontinued.

The Commission separates rate complaints seeking damages from carriers willing to pay from those where an initial carrier-shipper agreement is absent. The former must be filed by the carrier on what is termed the special docket, along with requests by carriers to charge rates different from those in the ICC schedule.

Special Docket Settlement and Rate Complaints Dealing with Carriers and Shippers

Special docket settlement arises from the fact that the ICC establishes tariffs applicable to carriers under certain circumstances, and no deviation may be made from the scheduled rates without permission from the Commission. If such tariffs are exceeded by carriers a claim for damages may result on the part of the shipper concerned. If the carrier and shipper are in agreement, the carrier files a petition to effect the agreement. On the other hand, there are many cases in which carriers wish to adjust existing schedules to the benefit of the shipper, for competitive and other purposes. In this instance the carrier will appeal on the special docket contending that the existing rate schedule is unreasonable in the particular situation involved. About half of the special docket cases are filed by the carriers on their own volition, the remaining through shipper complaints.

The Section of Rates and Informal Cases in the Bureau of Traffic handles complaints not in the special docket category. As a general rule this section attempts to settle informal cases through correspondence. Initially, a determination is made concerning the validity and importance of the complaint. Around 25 per cent of the complaints are dismissed as of insufficient importance. Such disposition, of an informal nature, is of importance to the complainant, the effect being the same as an adverse decision.

Complaints considered to be valid are sent to the carriers concerned; they, in turn, are given the opportunity to submit their answer, which is sent to the complainant. Through this give and take, in which the Commission staff participates, a settlement is usually reached. The decision, with supporting reasons, is sent to the parties involved. Normally the adjudicative process regarding informal complaints ends at this point, with the parties accepting informal disposition.

The development and significance of the Commission's settlement procedures in the informal complaint and special docket area is summed up by an ICC hearing examiner in the following way:

> In 1906, with the Hepburn Act giving it authority, . . . the Commission organized its Bureau of Informal Cases. Therein are handled letters, informal complaints, and special dockets, by the thousands at bureau level. . . . [L]et us examine . . . why it has worked well. Since 1906 the Bureau has been headed by a chief (fewer men have served it as chief than your fingers on one hand) who emulates . . . a *good administrator*. . . . The chief has at his aid, when he desires to use it, a so-called Board of Reference composed of such men as the Commission's Chief Counsel, Director, Bureau of Traffic, the Chief Examiner, Director of its Bureau of Inquiry, et al who participate in decisions of difficult cases of precedent-making character. In appropriate . . . cases they are referred to a division and sometimes to the Commission for decision on the record submitted informally as a complaint or special docket. Reparation in amounts approaching two million dollars per year has been awarded, in cases of that class, under this informal (almost unnoticed) procedure. Though practically unnoted so far as the public is concerned, it mills a large grist for shippers and carriers.[24]

This type of procedure illustrates so-called institutional decision-making, in which various staff groups participate in the investigation of a complaint as well as in the formulation of a final decision.

Aside from the informal complaints the Section of Rates and Informal Cases handles a large number of letters of a complaint nature which are not strictly classified as such. Much of the correspondence of this section relates to these complaint letters, which frequently deal with the application and interpretation of tariffs with respect to disputes that have developed between shippers and carriers, or among the carriers themselves. In such instances the informal views of the Commission are requested to avoid expensive formal litigation before the Commission or in the courts. In many instances "a disputed matter is submitted as to which the parties have stipulated that they will settle the matter on the basis of the informal view requested. Often this informal handling of disputes results in acceptance of the informal view by the parties without prior agreement to do so. It is safe to say that settlements involving considerable sums of money are achieved by this method, and that it is of great importance in avoiding formal litigation and in the settlement of disputes wherein the amounts involved do not warrant formal litigation." [25] This informal interpretative advice does not apply to future transactions, but rather to concrete controversies and, being informal, does not bind the Commission if such a dispute should reach the formal administrative hearing stage.

The significance of the informal complaint process before the ICC is evident from the accompanying table, which contrasts formal and informal complaints as well as complaint letters, in rate cases involving rail carriers.

ICC HANDLING OF FORMAL AND INFORMAL COMPLAINTS,
RAIL CARRIERS RATE CASES

Year	Formal complaints	Informal complaints	Complaint letters
1950	305	2,318	14,000
1955	227	1,631	13,000
1960	142	2,602	11,000

SOURCE: ICC Annual Reports.

It is evident that in the complaint area involving rail carrier rates the volume of adjudication sharply decreases as formality increases.

Service Complaints and Demurrage Disputes

Under section 1(11) of the Interstate Commerce Act carriers must furnish safe and adequate car service, including proper "use, control, supply, movement, distribution, exchange, interchange and return of locomotives, cars and other vehicles." [26] Based upon this provision the Commission receives numerous "service complaints" against carriers, as well as carrier complaints to the effect that consignees have not returned cars within the agreed time span or have not returned them in satisfactory condition. In the latter instance carriers will charge for the excess time involved before cars are returned, and in some cases demurrage disputes will develop involving the charge made by the carrier.

Although the Commission does not maintain records capable of producing the exact number of service complaints handled each year, it has estimated such complaints to be around 300 to 400. The number of demurrage disputes is considerably less, totaling 13 from November, 1951, through August, 1957.[27] In both types of complaint informal settlement is effected in about 98 per cent of the cases. About a third of the service complaints are dismissed for lack of jurisdiction. The techniques employed are a combination of correspondence, conference, and investigation, depending upon the needs of particular cases.

Complaints Involving Motor Carriers

Complaints relating to the operation of motor carriers can be divided into two classes: (1) those relating to applications for certificates of public convenience and necessity; (2) those involving other aspects of motor carrier operation, rates for instance. Preliminary hearings are conducted by examiners in most of the cases involving certificate complaints.

Service complaints involving motor carriers are handled by the field staff of the Bureau of Motor Carriers within the Commission. In fiscal 1960 this staff received 16,460 complaints and immediately disposed of 11,603 of them by letter and telephone. Investigations were conducted in 5,002 cases, and of these 4,005 were settled informally. In 997 cases investigations were made with a view to possible formal Commission or court proceedings.

Eventually, however, most of this latter category of case is settled informally.[28] In contrast to the volume of informal cases only 22 formal complaints involving motor carriers were filed during the same period.

Summary and Evaluation

The adjudicative activities of the ICC regarding damage and non-damage suits between shippers and carriers, service complaints and demurrage disputes, and the operation of motor carriers, provide yet another example of the predominance of informal adjudication in the administrative process. In some instances informal settlements number over 95 per cent. In all areas a substantial majority of the cases are settled by informal means.

The ICC, like the NLRB, deals more with groups than with individuals; hence the possibilities of arbitrary action in the informal realm are reduced. On the other hand most of the controversies do not involve large amounts, and are not of such great importance, that the parties involved would care to take the time and spend the money necessary to resort to formal proceedings. This gives to the administrators involved a form of sanction very useful in enforcement proceedings.

In general, practitioners before the ICC and others who have studied the agency[29] support the Commission's reliance upon informal procedure in adjudication. In many instances a plea is made for greater use of such procedure, to reduce the formal docket even more than is now the case. Regardless of the particular emphasis given to informal procedure, it is evident that at present the adjudicative procedure of the Commission cannot be conceptualized in terms of the adversary process.

THE SECURITIES AND EXCHANGE COMMISSION

Although the SEC is primarily concerned with the adjudication of application cases, a significant portion of its work involves settlement of complaints. The Commission is authorized to conduct investigations and pursue remedies regarding the violation of any act it administers. Its own remedies may be injunctive proceedings in District Courts, or formal proceedings before the

Commission. Cases involving criminal prosecution are transferred to the Department of Justice. In fiscal 1960 the Commission initiated 53 injunctive proceedings against 159 defendants; 39 were granted against 117 defendants. In the criminal realm, during the same year, 53 cases involving 281 defendants were referred to the Justice Department.

On the other hand, a large volume of complaint cases, usually involving SEC initiation of the complaint based upon information furnished from a variety of sources, are processed each year through informal methods. The Commission has described part of its complaint procedure in the following way:

> One of the principal sources of information upon which investigations are based is complaints from members of the public concerning the activities of persons involved in the offer and sale of securities. Information of this type is carefully studied and if it appears that violations of Federal securities laws may be involved an investigation is commenced. Other sources of information which may be of great help to the Commission in carrying out its enforcement responsibilities are national securities exchanges, brokerage firms, State and Canadian securities authorities, Better Business Bureaus, Chambers of Commerce, and the National Association of Securities Dealers, Inc. Information from these sources has been very helpful, for it comes from persons who are often familiar with the operation and applicability of Federal securities laws. Many investigations also result from processing of filings which are required to be made with the Commission. Many preliminary investigations disclose no violation of law or a violation due to misunderstanding or ignorance of the law. Where no harm to the public has resulted, it is a policy of the Commission to inform the offender of the violation and afford an opportunity to take steps to assure future compliance. Appropriate action is taken where such an offender fails to come promptly into compliance.[30]

The Commission receives a large number of complaint letters which, because they fail to indicate a reasonable possibility of a legal violation, are disposed of without investigation. This is the preinvestigative complaint stage. Although figures for recent

years have not been reported by the Commission, some idea
of the significance of this stage may be seen from the fact
that 10,100 complaint letters were received in fiscal 1951, whereas
during the same year only 1,582 new cases were listed for investigation.[31] Preinvestigative cases are handled through correspondence, because of lack of evidence sufficient to warrant an
investigation.

Within the investigative stage of a complaint the Commission
has established (1) preliminary and (2) docketed categories.
In preliminary cases, investigations are carried out informally
through correspondence and limited field work. Investigations
are always conducted privately, both to prevent frustration of
Commission efforts to secure evidence of violations, and to protect private parties that are innocent even though they may be
involved initially. In the words of the Commission, "many situations which are investigated ultimately develop facts which establish that no violation has occurred. To conduct such investigations
publicly would ordinarily result in hardship or embarrassment to
innocent persons and might affect the market for the securities in
question, resulting in injury to public investors. Many persons
have a tendency to be reluctant to furnish information concerning suspected violations if they think their personal affairs might
be publicized. The Commission's policy is designed to protect
both those who furnish information relating to securities transactions and the subjects of investigation against whom no violation ultimately is established." [32] This is a good illustration of the
way in which informal procedure aids the enforcement efforts of
regulatory agencies.

On the other hand, when a case is docketed for thorough investigation it is necessary in some instances for the Commission
to issue formal orders of investigation, "appointing members of
the staff as officers with power to issue subpoenas for the produc-
tion of documentary evidence, the appearance of witnesses and
the taking of testimony under oath. This step is taken only when
the investigations cannot be otherwise successfully completed,
such as when principals and others involved in the investigation
are uncooperative and the evidence can be adduced only through
the use of the subpoena power." [33] Regardless of the particular
type of method employed in the informal investigative complaint

stage, very few cases require further Commission action to bring about settlement. The investigative process becomes the adjudicative process.

The table indicates the extent of Commission activity in the

SEC INVESTIGATIONS OF POSSIBLE LEGAL VIOLATIONS

	Preliminary	*Docketed*	*Total*
Pending June 30, 1960	116	844	960
New cases	131	415	546
Transferred from preliminary		21	21
Total	247	1,280	1,527
Closed	103	277	380
Transferred to docketed	21		21
Pending 6-30-61	123	1,003	1,126

SOURCE: 1960 SEC Annual Report, p. 202.

investigative process. During the course of docketed investigations 155 formal orders of investigation were issued.

Summary and Evaluation

The complaint settlement procedure used by the SEC is clearly almost entirely informal in nature. If a complaint is not disposed of through correspondence at the preinvestigative stage, an informal or semiformal investigation is conducted which usually constitutes final adjudication, for the case under consideration is normally adjusted or dismissed in the course of the investigation.

The SEC has powerful sanctions, especially its ability to bring about severe hardships to private parties through publicizing the fact of investigation. Adverse publicity seriously hurts financial interests, particularly in the securities field, where satisfactory marketability of a stock is destroyed if there is any doubt at all about the company or individuals concerned. This sanction works to the benefit of the Commission in enforcement action, and encourages informal and confidential settlement of disputes. A similar effect was observed regarding SEC settlement of application cases, where far more is generally at stake financially than in the complaint case area. SEC informal settlement of complaints illustrates the extent of Commission discretion, and points out, once again, the complexity of the problem of administrative responsibility in the regulatory process.

THE FEDERAL COMMUNICATIONS COMMISSION
AND THE CIVIL AERONAUTICS BOARD

Complaints arise under the jurisdiction of the FCC with regard to such diverse areas as the regulation of common carriers by wire or radio (telephone and telegraph companies), interference with various forms of communication, and radio and television programming. The operation of the Field Engineering and Monitoring Division of the FCC which investigates and adjudicates interference complaints will be discussed at a later point as part of the "pure administrative process."

Complaints regarding the operation of common carriers, by which is meant any party other than those engaged in radio broadcasting "engaged as a common carrier for hire, in interstate or foreign communication by wire or radio or in interstate or foreign radio transmission of energy," [34] arise under Title II of the Communications Act of 1934. The act specifies that carriers must provide designated forms of service, must not engage in specified types of discrimination, must charge just and reasonable rates, and in general fulfill numerous conditions. Suspected violation of any of these provisions may cause a complaint to be filed with the Commission.

Upon receipt of a complaint, the Commission staff takes the question up with the respondent by correspondence, notifying the carrier of the complaint and asking that it either satisfy the complainant or tell the Commission of its inability to act. Formal proceedings are rarely used in the adjudication of complaint cases regarding the operations of common carriers.

Complaints Relating to Radio and Television Broadcasting

The Commission receives thousands of complaint letters each year concerning particular radio or television programs or performers. Very few of these complaints are taken seriously by the Commission, because of their obvious irresponsibility and lack of evidence of legal violation. About 10 per cent of the complaints are investigated and followed up, with a view to settlement. In this area the FCC has powerful informal sanctions working in its favor, for the constant theoretical threat of license revocation at renewal time is always present, although in fact the FCC has never carried out a threat to revoke a license because of programming. In 1961 the new chairman of the FCC (Newton Minow) threatened to take a long look at station license renewal applications if the stations did not conform to public service programming criteria. In this way Commission action in the application case area affects the settlement of complaints, for station owners are reluctant to take a chance, however small, on the suspension of their licenses; thus if a complaint arises in the programming field that accuses a station of violating FCC standards the mere notification of the respondent of the fact of the complaint would result in immediate settlement in many cases. In this regard the *Wall Street Journal* commented on June 29, 1961:

> A few months ago Federal Communications Commission Chairman Newton Minow threatened that unless the TV industry improved program quality the agency in the future might refuse to renew broadcast licenses. But license renewal applications from stations in Arkansas, Louisiana and Mississippi, the first to be acted upon since the warning, are being processed in the usual routine fashion, say station owners.
>
> "Our license was renewed without a question," states the manager of a Mississippi station, adding that the station has made no significant changes in its programming. Station owners in Little Rock, New Orleans, Meridian, Miss., and Alexandria, La., report similar experiences. "I don't think he (Minow) knows yet what his standards are," says one operator. Another labels Minow's threats as just "New Frontier overenthusiasm."
>
> But some station owners worry. A Shreveport station adds public service programs and plans more because, says the manager, "we value our licenses." [35]

This illustrates the way in which administrative policies become involved and substantially shape the adjudicative process. The fact that agencies have policy power enhances their ability to secure informal settlement, if meaningful sanctions are present.

The Civil Aeronautics Board

The CAB divides its complaint categories into (1) those relating generally to its rules and regulations regarding airman certificates, certificates of air worthiness, air carrier operation certificates, and the like; and (2) those regarding air service. The former, certificate complaints, generally involve safety enforcement proceedings disciplinary in nature; the latter type of complaint falls into the category of "economic enforcement" and pertains to enforcement of the economic provisions of the Federal Aviation Act of 1958, involving standards of competition, service, and so forth.

In the field of safety enforcement there are statutory requirements for notice and hearing before disciplinary action may be taken by the CAB; the Board has construed this to require an opportunity for hearing rather than a necessity for hearing. Insofar as possible, an attempt is made to dispose of this type of case informally. After the Administrative Procedure Act of 1946 the Board extended informality in this area by delegating to its examiners the authority to make initial decisions which became final in the absence of exceptions filed by the respondent. In the first year of the operation of this procedure, fiscal 1947, 342 out of 550 dispositions were decided by examiners on a consent basis. In 1948, of 776 cases closed, over 90 per cent were on the basis of the examiner's decision. By 1950 the percentage closed in this way was increased to 95. In 1959, out of 640 cases 524 were settled on the basis of the examiner's decision without review, which is slightly less than 90 per cent.[36]

The accompanying table contains the activities of the CAB in safety enforcement for fiscal 1959. Approximately 66 per cent of these proceedings are handled informally and without hearing. This is of particular interest, considering the personal importance of many of these cases.

An examination of the service complaint area before the CAB illustrates an even greater predominance of informal procedure than is used in safety enforcement. Another table, herewith, indi-

CAB SAFETY ENFORCEMENT DURING FISCAL 1959

1. Proceedings pending July 1, 1958	342
2. Proceedings initiated	422
Total	764
3. Disposition (249 with hearings):	
Certificates revoked	143
Certificates suspended	358
Medical review granted	41
Medical review denied	8
Proceedings dismissed or terminated	64
Proceedings withdrawn and completed	
by administrative action	38
Total	652
Pending 6-30-59	112

SOURCE: 1959 CAB Annual Report, p. 49.

cates the work load of the Board in this area for fiscal 1959. The Board has noted with respect to these proceedings that "all these complaints are handled initially on an informal basis and

CAB CASE LOAD IN THE AREA OF ECONOMIC ENFORCEMENT—1959

Item	Pending 7-1-58	Instituted	Completed	Pending 6-30-59
1. Informal cases	409	1,321	1,152	578
2. Formal Board proceedings and court actions	52	30	30	52
3. Investigations	175	375	419	131
4. Special enforcement projects	39	16	12	43
Total	675	1,742	1,613	804

SOURCE: 1959 CAB Annual Report, p. 33.

a great majority of them are concluded to the satisfaction of the complainants. In the event that violations disclosed by these complaints continue despite warnings and opportunities to achieve voluntary compliance, formal enforcement proceedings are instituted to stop such violations."[37] In contrast to the volume of informal economic cases before the CAB in 1959, only

11 of the formal proceeding cases were terminated by trial examiners, eight being settled through consent.[38] In other words, even though formal proceedings may be indicated this does not mean a formal hearing was utilized.

The purpose of this chapter has been to describe and analyze settlement methods used by characteristic and important administrative agencies. From the examination of these agencies a valid composite picture of the general operation of administrative agencies emerges. Several important conclusions regarding administrative adjudication may be stated.

First, in contrast to the application case area discussed in the preceding chapter, the need to adjudicate complaint cases is more pervasive in the administrative process. Most agencies engaged in regulation exercise important complaint settlement functions.

Second, similar techniques of informal settlement are used in each of the agencies examined. Informal conferences and correspondence between the parties to a dispute and the agency concerned usually suffice to settle the issues in controversy. Frequently, initial decisions regarding the validity of a case, which may result in dismissal or withdrawal, are determinative. And in many instances the initial agency decision of a substantive nature, for example, the determination by the Internal Revenue Service that a deficiency exists in a particular tax return, is generally not challenged by the private party concerned because of the time, expense, and uncertainty involved. The stipulation, an informal agreement between the government and the private party, has been an administrative settlement technique of particular importance, as illustrated in the operation of the Federal Trade Commission and the Internal Revenue Service. The operation of the FTC also reflects the importance of the admissive answer and consent order settlement techniques operative at the formal level. The latter procedure has now replaced the stipulation before the FTC. It should be noted also that informal settlements are frequently effected "administratively" by agency staffs during the course of investigations.

Third, the systems that have been established to provide for expeditious informal settlement vary to a considerable extent within the administrative process; however, in no case is the system of informal adjudication haphazard. The Internal Revenue Service, for example, has established an elaborate system for informal adjudication, composed of an extensive initial informal conference level and an appellate stage which may informally review initial decisions upon the request of the individual or group concerned. Substantive and procedural standards have been developed by the IRS as a guide to conferees. In other agencies informal settlement systems, although perhaps not as elaborate as that of the IRS, nevertheless are carefully organized and the best organized systems have been established by those agencies (such as the IRS) which must process a large volume of cases. In many agencies it has been found that informal adjudication effects the purposes of the enabling statutes involved, and thus settlement procedures are carefully defined.

Fourth, the reasons for extensive administrative reliance upon informal procedure in adjudication vary, but generally can be outlined in the following terms: (1) the volume of cases coming before these agencies; (2) the need for speed, to aid effective governmental regulation and to protect the parties involved from prolonged litigation; (3) the expense inherent in formal proceedings; (4) the need to avoid ill-feelings among private parties which frequently stems from formal adversary hearings, in order to promote the goals of particular statutes, such as, for example, the National Labor Relations Act; (5) the need to avoid the publicity that frequently attends formal proceedings in order to protect private interests from punishment unjustified in terms of the statutes involved; (6) the need to employ *expertise,* through flexible investigative techniques; for at least in theory this last is not possible in an adversary proceeding which requires a decision to be based on the record made by the parties. These factors combine in various ways in the operation of administrative agencies in the complaint case area, necessitating the use of informal adjudicative procedure.

Fifth, a problem of administrative responsibility exists with respect to the informal adjudicative activities of all of the agencies that have been considered. The problem, which is essentially one of administrative justice, varies in degree in different agencies. Where persons are directly affected in their individual capacities, as, say, before the Internal Revenue Service, a particularly acute problem is present because of the lack of balanced resources between the agency and the parties coming within its jurisdiction. Of course formal procedure is predicated upon the equality of the parties involved, so that the record produced will bring out all of the facts, both adverse and favorable, to each party. In administrative law, upon judicial review, justice theoretically depends upon an equal presentation of the case by both sides. Where agencies act as judges as well as represent or act as complainants, they have considerable unchecked discretion when they are dealing with individuals who essentially must settle informally. On the other hand, where powerful groups are involved, not only are they better able to protect themselves, but the possibility of appeal is frequently present.

Finally, there are important areas in administrative law where private parties must submit to agency decisions made informally because of the existence of powerful administrative sanctions. For example, many parties involved in a dispute with the FCC will avoid the risk of license revocation and settle informally in accordance with the wishes of the government. The need to avoid publicity, which is necessarily adverse, precludes meaningful appeal even to the formal administrative process in the operation of the Securities and Exchange Commission. Where such sanctions exist, private parties usually will accept initial agency decisions. These factors complement those mentioned above necessitating informal adjudication. Thus administrative complaint adjudication is generally informal in nature, and frequently the advantage lies with the government. The significance of this in terms of the problem of securing administrative justice will be analyzed in the concluding chapter.

Chapter V

THE PURE ADMINISTRATIVE PROCESS

All administrative adjudication is characterized by its technicality; however, it is meaningful to give separate treatment to certain forms of adjudication where decisions are made almost solely on the basis of technical rules and evidence, and where the opportunity for adversary hearings in any form is eliminated. This area of technical adjudication will be designated the "pure administrative process" and will be illustrated by means of references to several of the more important agencies engaged in such adjudication.[1]

It is necessary, first of all, to realize that the pure administrative process is part of the informal process. It is a type of informal adjudication, where opposing points of view are not resolved on the basis of argument presented by applicants, complainants, or respondents, but rather by administrative reference to technical data. Such data may be, for example, of a medical nature, or it may stem from complex administrative regulations based upon statutory provisions. In either case adjudication is not generally open to question by lay members of the public, who in most instances have little understanding of the issues. On the other hand, there is nothing absolute about *expertise,* and one could argue that the most vigorous conflicts of view are to be found among professional groups or other so-called "experts." This is true; however, no matter how heated a controversy may become among experts, the fact is that in vast areas of administration decisions are made on the basis of technical considerations without involving lay individuals in an adversary proceeding or in a meaningful give and take of ideas. Insofar as administrative standards are involved which establish experts to the exclusion or without the existence of significant outside expert groups, the pure administrative process is strengthened. Here administrative specialization equals *expertise.* For example, any administrative standard involving medical evidence may easily be challenged because of the existence of a significant medical group outside

145

of the administrative process. On the other hand, ICC inspection decisions involving the safety of locomotives will not be so easily challenged because, although various kinds of engineers can be found to testify apart from those employed by the Commission, the technical standards in this area have been formulated primarily by the ICC, which has discretion in interpretation. There is no substantial body of scientific knowledge concerning locomotive safety, apart from that possessed by ICC experts; thus to a considerable extent the only experts are the administrative experts.

Examples of pure administrative adjudication are found throughout the administrative process. This chapter will deal briefly with examples to be found in the Veterans Administration and the Bureau of Old Age and Survivors Insurance within the Social Security Administration; and with certain aspects of the work of the FCC, FTC, and ICC.

THE VETERANS ADMINISTRATION AND THE BUREAU OF OLD AGE AND SURVIVORS INSURANCE

The VA and the Bureau of Old Age and Survivors Insurance illustrate benefit adjudication by administrative agencies. These agencies are in an unusual position because they have been established to protect and advance the interests of the very individuals whose cases they must adjudicate. The agency, in this field, becomes the advocate of the private party making application for particular benefits; with limited resources, it must choose among applicants in accordance with legal and in many instances medical criteria. It is in this process of decision-making that adjudication is involved, for the legal rights of specific individuals must be determined. In this area the applicant generally will rely upon the "expert" determination of the agency, although in a relatively few cases avenues of informal appeal are used.

The Veterans Administration provides the best example of the pure administrative process in the benefit field. The VA has jurisdiction over 81 million persons, if both veterans and their families are counted; there are over 22.5 million veterans. Thus this agency affects potentially about 45 per cent of the total population of the country.[2] The benefit categories are varied and complex. They include, under various congressional statutes: compensation for service-connected disability or death; dependency and indemnity compensation; vocational rehabilitation for service-connected disability; education and training; war orphans' educational assistance; guaranty or insurance of home, farm, and business loans, and, under certain conditions, direct home loans; United States Government and National Service Life Insurance; insurance indemnity; hospitalization; domiciliary care; outpatient medical and dental care for service-connected disability; prosthetic and other appliances; special housing for certain seriously disabled veterans; automobiles or other conveyances for certain disabled veterans; World War I adjusted service certificates; a guardianship program for the protection of estates derived from Veterans Administration benefits paid to incompetent or minor beneficiaries; burial allowances; and burial flags. In addition the Veterans Administration administers the insurance section of the Soldiers' and Sailors' Civil Relief Act for persons in the active military service.[3]

VA Organization for Adjudication

Because of the large volume of cases involved, informal procedure is used at all adjudicative levels in the VA. The complexity and volume of cases results in the emphasis of institutional decision-making, which varies in accordance with the case category under consideration. Uniformly *contact personnel* participate directly in the processing of all types of cases, and for the average veteran they are the focal point in the adjudicative process. The VA has accurately stated:

To the individual veteran, his dependent, beneficiary, representative or other interested person, trained contact personnel are the point of personal contact with the Veterans Administration, providing uniform information relative to participation in various veterans' benefits; assisting claimants in the preparation, development, and submission of applications for benefits that are *appropriate* and *complete* with necessary supporting evidence; and representing claimants upon their request before rating agencies, boards, or officials of the Veterans Administration authorized to take determinative action on matters pertaining to veterans' benefits.[4] During fiscal 1960 contact personnel conducted 4.6 million personal interviews with applicants and assisted over 3 million additionally through telephone interviews.[5] Each year, over 1 million applications are prepared in the contact offices, and in over 100,-000 cases contact personnel appear before rating groups within the VA. These are not simply "routine" cases, particularly in the latter instance where the rating received, determining the extent of disability, or whether or not a claim can be made at all under the regulations of the agency, affects the remuneration received.

It is interesting to postulate the extent to which contact personnel actually make determinative decisions in the adjudicative process. Although in theory the contact staff cannot or should not influence adjudication, the fact is that in a number of instances they make important initial decisions concerning the acceptability of applications for benefits that are generally not challenged by the applicants. Of course in most cases they will try to help the applicant to secure benefits from the agency; therefore it is reasonable to assume that more invalid applications are accepted than valid applications rejected. Nevertheless, a certain amount of important discretion is exercised even at this initial level. And even though an application is accepted, the contact personnel shape the nature of the request that will eventually reach those having final power of disposition.

Aside from the key role played by contact personnel in all case categories, each type of application to the VA is subject to a different form of adjudication. The only common thread is the virtual elimination of the hearing process, with the exception of appellate cases. Even at the appellate level hearings, when they are held, are informal.

In the area of disability compensation applications, within each regional office an adjudication division and medical personnel participate. After screening by contact personnel, an application is sent first to the authorization unit within the adjudication division, which determines basic eligibility for monetary benefits and obtains initial evidence necessary for proper adjudication.

Claim development of this type is generally handled through correspondence, although in rare instances field examination may be used. Once eligibility has been established, and this is a critical part of the adjudicative process, the case is turned over to "adjudicators" within the division, who complete the gathering of evidence relevant to a particular case. This is so that the rating board, which has the determinative power in the adjudication of disability claims, may make its decision with a minimum of wasted effort. Through the work of the adjudicators the necessity of further hearing before the rating board is generally eliminated. At the initial adjudicative stage—that is, before the case goes to the rating board—oral presentation of evidence is rare; hearings, if held at all, are informal.

The rating board has final authority to determine service-connection of disability, to evaluate and rate the disability under consideration, to determine competency of claimants, and to determine whether or not insanity affects entitlement. These are issues of the highest technical complexity, involving extensive medical knowledge. Because of the *expertise* involved, rating boards are composed of three specialists who judge cases coming before them from the standpoint of their particular specialties. A physician examines and judges the medical aspects of the case; a lawyer determines the legal problems, if any, presented by the case; and finally an occupational specialist judges the case as a representative of the lay point of view. In this manner rating boards attempt to focus the requisite expertness upon cases requiring expert opinion for effective judgment. They also reflect the need for institutional decision-making with regard to complex cases; an institutional process has "pointed-up" the case for the rating board, which itself must represent a group decision. Each of the rating specialists must participate in the decision according to the regulations of the agency.[6]

Although the rating board has final adjudicative authority, the disposition of the case has been largely determined beforehand. After the basic non-medical facts of a case have been established the decision in the disability area must be based primarily upon medical evidence; therefore, it is proper to consider the medical examination itself as part of the adjudicative process. As a general rule the physician on the rating board does not himself examine the applicant but rather reviews the medical record that has already been established by the medical and psychiatric units within the regional office.

The predominance of medical *expertise* in the adjudicative process of the VA is also evident with regard to the disposition of applications for outpatient medical and dental treatment, where patients are treated by VA physicians in the regional office, as well as with regard to applications for hospitalization and domiciliary care. This area also includes applications for special housing, automobiles, or the like, involving disabled veterans. Basic eligibility for outpatient treatment and hospitalization is established by the regional office adjudication division primarily on the basis of service-connection, although nonservice-connected cases may also be given treatment on the basis of need, provided all eligible service-connected cases have been treated. The most important substantive adjudication in these areas is in fact carried out by the medical units determining the nature of the malady, its history (thus influencing decisions concerning service-connection), and what type of treatment is to be given to the applicant. In this area, as in the area of disability compensation cases, the adjudicative process is far removed from the individuals concerned, and decisions rest primarily upon technical criteria.

The VA is characterized by pure administrative adjudication not only in the medical area, but also with respect to applications in the education, training, and vocational rehabilitation area, and in the loan guaranty field. In both these areas, applications are handled by special divisions at the regional office level. The education program, which was once receiving over 2 million applications a year, has been reduced to a point where less than 30,000 applications are being processed each year. In these areas as well as others, adjudication is frequently based upon the facts submitted in the application. Beyond this evidence is obtained and tested, if necessary, informally. A final area of pure adjudication within the VA's jurisdiction is composed of various insurance programs. It operates the third largest ordinary life insurance program in the world. Although much of the work in the insurance field is routine, a small number of adjudicative decisions must be rendered concerning such things as eligibility of claimants, amount of benefits, and so on, for particular cases.

Provisions for Appeal

It is provided by law that "all decisions rendered by the Administrator of Veterans' Affairs . . . shall be final and conclusive on all questions of law and fact, and no other official or court of the United States shall have jurisdiction to review by mandamus or otherwise any such decision."[7] Based upon this provision the courts have repeatedly held that decisions of the Veterans Administration are not subject to judicial review, with the exception of claims on insurance contracts.[8] The latter are less than 1 per cent of the appeals workload. Appeal may be made on an intra-agency basis to the Board of Veterans Appeals, and all questions on claims involving benefits are subject to review by this board. Usually, the decision of the lower adjudicative body will be upheld unless new and material evidence is introduced or error indicated.

Generally, over 50 per cent of the appellate cases are decided without hearing. This may be observed in the table presented here. The appellate process begins at the field level, where approximately 20 per cent of the appellate cases are settled without the necessity of further action. Regional or district office per-

BOARD OF VETERANS APPEALS—CASE LOAD

	Fiscal 1959	Fiscal 1960
1. Appealed cases settled	36,302	39,136
2. Hearing held	16,982	17,798

SOURCE: 1960 VA Annual Report, p. 107.

sonnel may act as a hearing agency for the board, where this is more convenient and desirable to the claimant. Where hearings are held they are informal, and, as the VA has indicated, "strict rules of evidence are not invoked and considerable freedom in argument is permitted, except that argument or testimony must be relevant to the issue involved."[9] Transcripts are made of hearings and become part of the claimant's file.

Statistical Summary—VA

To illustrate the present-day significance and scope of pure administrative adjudication carried out by the VA, the next table computes a typical one-year case load in the more important categories. The figures are averages for the years 1950 to 1961. The case load of the VA is so great that after the Second World

TYPICAL ONE-YEAR CASE LOAD IN DESIGNATED CATEGORIES—VA

Application category	Volume of cases adjudicated
1. Guaranty or insurance of loans	600,344
2. Outpatient dental treatment	200,000
3. Hospitalization and domiciliary care	1,000,000
4. Outpatient medical treatment	200,000
5. Education and training	500,000
6. Disability compensation and pension	70,000
7. Death compensation and pension	30,000
Total	2,600,344

SOURCE: VA Annual Reports.

War, when benefit applications were particularly high, regional offices were processing, separately, up to 3,600 cases per day. During this period the VA received in one year, for example, as many as 2,882,995 applications in the education and training category alone. The need for expeditious procedure is evident.

The Bureau of Old Age and Survivors Insurance

A further, and highly significant, example of pure administrative adjudication in the benefit area is provided by the Bureau of Old-Age and Survivors Insurance within the Social Security Administration. In general, the adjudication of social security (and disability) applications involves determinations with regard to: (1) qualifying conditions; and (2) factors resulting in termination or suspension of benefits. A unique aspect of adjudication, both in the VA and in the BOASI, is that in most instances it is a continuing process, for benefit rights may be terminated if factors affecting an individual change after initial favorable adjudication.

Within the category of qualifying conditions, the initial adjudication is based, for example, on whether or not the applicant has been employed for a designated period in "covered" employment. The period of employment, the amount of earnings, conditions of relationship, dependency, and so on, affect the determination. The applicant must furnish proof, the acceptability of which is carefully defined in administrative regulations, regarding his identity, age, and other conditions legally involved in the determination of particular benefits. With regard to the termination or suspension of benefits factors such as reëmployment, death, divorce, marriage, failure to send children to school, and the like, are considered in the adjudicative process.

In 1954 disability "freeze" provisions were added to the Social Security Act by which the insured status of workers is preserved in case of long-term or total disability. In 1956 amendments were passed which extended benefits to children of insured workers over the age of eighteen if they become disabled before reaching that age. To have his status "frozen," an individual must have worked in covered employment for at least five out of the ten years preceding the beginning of his disability, and one and a half of the years worked must have been during the three years immediately preceding the disability. Congress specified that disability determinations under the new Social Security provisions were to be charged to those state agencies approved under the Vocational Rehabilitation Act which administer a federal-state program of aid to the permanently and totally disabled, or to other appropriate state bodies. In most instances state vocational rehabilitation agencies have been designated by the governors to make disability determinations. The BOASI is to negotiate with the designated state agency an agreement providing for uniform adjudicative standards, state accountability for federal funds, personnel standards, and other relevant administrative details. The Bureau handles cases not covered by state agreements.

The BOASI established a new Division of Disability Operations with skilled technical personnel to review state determinations in the disability area, and to make direct adjudicative decisions where no state agreement existed. Applicants seeking benefits apply at the appropriate district office, which compiles a case file to be forwarded to the legal adjudicative body, whether state or federal. The problem of maintaining a coördinated program is therefore particularly difficult because of the many units involved.

All of the adjudication involved in these case categories is highly expert in nature. With respect to regular BOASI adjudication, the *expertise* involves a thorough knowledge of administrative regulations and the ability to compute benefits from basic information. In this area the information is gathered by district office personnel, and benefits are computed on electronic equipment. In the disability field, it is medical *expertise* that is frequently determinative. The adversary process is nonexistent, as it would not fulfill informational needs and would defeat the underlying assumptions of a benefit agency, which is predicated upon the belief that benefit programs should be administered with sympathy and understanding and in no case should applicants consider themselves as adversaries in relation to the government.

The primary adjudicative unit within the BOASI is the district office. At the present time there are approximately 600 such offices, to which power has been delegated to make initial determinations regarding the rights of claimants to receive benefits. Claims and field representatives have been carefully trained to handle this type of adjudication, which essentially takes place through informal conferences or interviews at the district office level. The Bureau's earnings records determine available benefits, once basic eligibility has been established. The claims representatives assist claimants at the same time they make adjudicative decisions. Upon obtaining wage records, the administrative determination consists of three elements: (1) whether or not the claimant is entitled to the claim; (2) the amount of the benefits if entitlement is established; (3) the month in which benefits begin (in some instances benefits are paid on a retroactive basis).

Of course a great deal of the work of the BOASI is routine, but this should not obscure the fact that judgments must frequently be made determinative of private rights. A former acting assistant manager of a BOASI district office noted this in reviewing the activities of field personnel:

An interview with a claimant is, or should be, intensively directed toward establishing certain facts as to age, relationship, and employment. The account-number interview is designed to provide positive identification and establish any work history. The handling of discrepancies in wage reports, particularly in controversial cases, necessitates a clear showing of the facts as to wages and periods of employment. Often less tangible factors in the realm of human relationships must be ascertained, such as the extent of control of one individual over another's activities. The fact-finding process is not confined to the field assistant, or claims interviewer, or wage record investigator. Everyone in a field office is concerned, directly or indirectly, with the evaluation of evidence in one form or another. . . . The facts we have established must be presented to the area, central, or accounting operations offices in such a manner that there can be no doubt as to the appropriateness of the action that will follow.[10]

With respect to evidence presented at the district office level the same official noted:

The evidence which we are expected to develop is either primary or secondary. It may be established either through testimony (statements made by witnesses under legal sanction) or by documents, or acquired by personal first-hand observation or examination. The rules of evidence are the maxims which the sagacity and experience of ages have established as the best means of discriminating truth from error, and of contracting as far as possible the dangerous power of judicial discretion. We recognize that, so far as possible, we should use the best evidence rule commonly applied by the court, which is, briefly, "the original document is the best evidence." Because we are not limited by rules of procedure established for court use, we are free to consider any fact however presented which may have the effect of including the inference that another fact does or does not exist. In a field office we are continually reviewing evidence and other facts which lead us to conclusions similar to those which a legal tribunal would draw from the same set of facts.[11]

The BOASI has attempted to balance the personal and institutional elements in its adjudicative process. Because of the large scale of its operations a considerable portion of each decision is based upon technical and mechanical computation. For example, "in each 3-month period during 1955 the Division of Accounting Operations will record the opening of about 1 million new social security accounts, credit to individual records 53 million wage items received from 4 million employers and 1.2 million earnings reports from the self-employed, and compute 525,000 benefits on the basis of the earnings records of covered workers." [12] Regardless of the mechanical and electronic aspects of decision-making, Christgau, writing as Director of the BOASI, noted that:

> When individuals come in to apply for benefits, they are usually facing a critical period in their lives emotionally and economically—for the worker, retirement or disability; for his family, the death of the husband and father. Not unnaturally, their ability to cope with formal, impersonal instructions is at a low ebb. Yet they must understand instructions about responsibility for reporting events that would terminate their benefits or suspend them. The Bureau has found, as well, that beneficiaries get payments faster when there has been face-to-face discussion to obtain the facts necessary to support a claim.[13]

It is this need for "friendly adjudication" that is unique to benefit agencies.

The adjudication of disability claims involves greater discretion but is nevertheless highly expert in nature. Medical knowledge is determinative in this area, both in setting standards and in final adjudication. Private physicians acting within the framework of standards set by the BOASI in conjunction with state agencies have important power in the adjudicative process. Medical evidence may be gathered from a number of sources, including government files maintained by such agencies as the VA, to support a disability claim. Although the program of providing disability benefits was not started until 1954, by October 1957 over 900,000 disability applications had been filed with district offices. Of these, 620,000 had been adjudicated, 34,000 of which were for children's benefits. In the children's category 30,000 were adjudicated favorably to the applicants; however, only 324,000 of the applications by workers were granted, representing 55 per cent. In many cases of denial it was found that the disability, however severe, did not prevent the applicant from engaging in gainful employment.[14] The extent of pure administrative adjudication in the disability field can be visualized in the accompanying tables:

DISABILITY ALLOWANCES AND DENIALS SINCE 1955

Year	Worker allowances	Worker denials	Childhood allowances	Childhood denials
1. 1955	57,221	36,310		
2. 1956	149,823	155,875		
3. 1957	165,003	125,720	36,267	4,873
4. 1958	184,476	204,110	21,273	5,544
5. 1959	178,952	146,325	34,718	5,745
Total	735,475	668,340	92,258	16,162

SOURCE: Social Security Bulletin, Annual Statistical Supplement, 1959, p. 61.

REASONS FOR WORKER DISABILITY DENIALS IN 1959

Reasons for denial	No.	%
1. Failed to meet quarters-of-coverage requirement at any time	1,530	1.0
2. Not disabled at latest time quarters-of-coverage requirements met	29,270	20.0
3. Failed to meet medical standards for disability	85,925	58.7
4. Met medical standards but able to engage in gainful activity	3,970	2.7
5. Failed to furnish sufficient evidence	19,040	13.0
6. Failed to meet requirements of 6 months continuous disability	3,335	2.3
7. Other	3,255	2.3
Total	146,325	100.0

SOURCE: Social Security Bulletin, Annual Statistical Supplement, 1959, p. 68.

Provisions for Reconsideration and Appeal—BOASI

In all cases where an initial determination is adverse to the claimant he is informed of his right to reconsideration, hearing, or appeal.[15] Reconsideration is undertaken by the administrative unit responsible for the initial determination. A request for reconsideration does not prejudice claimants' rights to a hearing after an adverse reconsidered determination has been made. A reconsideration involves both the evidence and the law of the case. It is, in a sense, a trial *de novo,* although initial investigative work is not repeated. New evidence may be presented by claimants at this initial appellate level, which does not, however, involve a hearing. Decisions are made strictly on the record.

Aside from provisions for reconsideration, claimants may obtain a hearing before a referee designated by an Appeals Council independent of the Bureau, although under unusual circumstances a member of the Council or a regional director may conduct such hearings. As a general rule, these hearings are entirely informal and are usually held in district office facilities. Under the terms of the Social Security Act the Social Security Administration has discretion in the determination of its procedural rules; however, claimants must be given the opportunity for a hearing on appeal. Specific procedure was not designated for such hearings; therefore, the BOASI is permitted to utilize informal procedure throughout its adjudicative process. At the outset, the appellate system of the Bureau was established on an independent basis, principally because the original Social Security Board felt that there was need for specialization in this area and because independent appellate systems were accepted in countries with mature social insurance systems.[16]

From the very beginning of the appellate system the Bureau has consulted informally with appellants at the district office level before a formal appeal is made. The purpose of these conferences is to clarify disputed points, to advise the claimant concerning evidence needed for appeal, and to initiate the proper steps for filing. Originally it was felt that informal consultation of this type would clarify any substantial matters in dispute and thereby aid adjudicative efficiency by focusing the subsequent hearing upon real issues in dispute. District office personnel in these cases act in a manner similar to VA contact personnel; they are the advocates for claimants. At the same time, a case may be settled at this level through informal acceptance of staff explanations for decisions that have been made.

Once the case reaches a referee on appeal the procedure utilized continues to be informal. In this respect the original goals of the Social Security Board regarding the appellate process are relevant:

> It is evident that the hearing in old-age and survivors insurance cases should be conducted in the simplest and most understandable manner possible. The Board is explicitly given authority to disregard the rules of evidence developed by courts, and there are many other aspects of a judicial proceeding which should be avoided. There is no need for the questioning of witnesses by counsel who "turn the witness over" from one to the other, for formal objections and exceptions to actions of the presiding officer or, in ordinary cases, for the cross-examination of witnesses. Cross-examination will not be possible in respect to reports and other evidence offered in written form. . . .
>
> The corollary that the hearing should be guided largely by the referee seems a sound one. In other words, he should not be an umpire between contending parties but, rather, a social agent whose function is to guide the hearing, observe the witnesses, and develop all the facts necessary to reach a just decision, and in so doing to build up a record upon the disputed points which will be adequate to sustain a decision in the case.[17]

For the most part, this framework is followed, and a great deal of discretion both as to procedure and as to the ultimate decision to be made, is given to the referee.

Summary

Both the VA and the Bureau of Old-Age and Survivors Insurance illustrate pure administrative adjudication in the benefit field. Most of the adjudication carried out by these agencies is highly technical in nature, and claimants are never involved in an adversary process, although informal proceedings of various types are used at both the initial and appellate levels of adjudication. Opportunity for formal hearings is entirely absent, the reasons for this being the nature of benefit agencies, which are designed to help claimants rather than to function in an adversary role, and the technical nature of decision-making, which precludes an adversary process of proof. The high volume of cases, moreover, necessitates informal institutional decision-making. The VA adjudicates approximately 2.5 million claims each year, and in 1959 the BOASI case volume was in excess of this figure. The VA dispenses over $5 billion in benefits each year, whereas the BOASI dispensed over $10 billion in benefits in 1959. The significance of these agencies in the determination of individual rights as well as in the over-all economic picture is clear.

THE FCC, FTC, AND ICC

The FCC, FTC, and ICC will be considered as remaining illustrations of pure administrative adjudication to indicate the nature of this area in a nonbenefit but regulatory field. Technical adjudication, without opportunity for hearing in any formal sense, is present in regulatory agencies in both the complaint and application case fields.

In the FCC, the Field Engineering and Monitoring Bureau illustrates pure administrative adjudication. This bureau is charged with the responsibility of settling complaints about radio interference, inspection of various types of radio installations to secure conformity to Commission standards, and with the adjudication of applications for radio operator licenses. In 1960 the Commission noted regarding the bureau that:

> Twenty-four establishments in key cities are designated as district offices, 5 as sub-offices and 2 as marine offices. Ten primary monitoring stations provide 24-hour-a-day technical and noncensorship surveillance of the spectrum. Eight secondary or backup stations increase the monitoring range and coverage. The 2 TV mobile units bring precise measurement equipment to the "door" of video stations. The Commission's enforcement staff, employing 42 investigative, 9 test, and 2 microwave cars, makes specialized inspections, signal analysis, investigations of unlicensed stations, and solutions of

interference cases. Over 50,000 personal contacts of home and industry installations were made during the year.[18] The Commission inspects all new FM and AM broadcast stations (including TV stations), as well as established stations, to secure compliance with administrative regulations which mostly involve technical engineering standards. New stations show a 30 per cent deficiency rate, whereas established stations have a deficiency rate in excess of 64 per cent. The most frequent deficiencies concern "inaccurate or missing indicating instruments, failure of transmitters to meet construction and safety (high voltage) requirements, lack of acceptable performance measurements, inability to maintain operating power within tolerance and lack of minimum operator compliance."[19] Needless to say, such cases are adjusted "administratively" during the course of inspections. The technical and unchallengeable nature of the regulations preclude any meaningful give and take between the government and licensees. In a similar vein, the FCC carries out technical inspections and investigations concerning radio operations on ships of certain classes, in taxicabs, in private aircraft, and elsewhere. Technical adjudication in this field involves interference complaints as well as application standards. Wherever radio sending apparatus in any form is used a license must be obtained and FCC standards must be met.

Another significant area in which the FCC carries out technical adjudication is with regard to commercial radio operators. In 1960 there were 329,000 applications for such licenses, which are processed through an examination procedure. The adjudicative determination is made from the results of the examination, which is mostly technical in nature. In a very few instances the Commission takes disciplinary action against operators who fail to meet standards. Although one may consider an area such as this completely routine, the fact is that the FCC has discretion in setting the criteria of examination, which, once established, are enforceable without question. Such procedure may not be particularly significant in an isolated area, yet a considerable portion of administrative determinations are made on this basis.

The statistics of the Field Engineering and Monitoring Bureau for 1960 indicate the quantitative significance of such adjudication. The qualitative significance is clear.

FCC FIELD INSPECTION STATISTICS—1960

Compulsory ship stations:	
Authorized	5,370
Inspections made	4,533
Violation notices served	1,369
Violations corrected during inspection	2,648
Certificates of compliance issued	3,020
Broadcast stations:	
Authorized	11,179
Inspections made	1,518
Violation notices served	980
Other radio stations (including aircraft,	
excluding ship and amateur):	
Authorized	333,684
Inspections made	6,592
Violation notices served	1,780
Notices of unlicensed operation	842

SOURCE: 1960 FCC Annual Report, p. 131.

Apart from this form of adjudication through field inspections, the FCC in 1960 completed adjudication of the large volume of radio operator license cases noted above and settled 23,985 interference complaint cases. It is evident that pure administrative adjudication in a regulatory area is similar to that in benefit areas with respect to (1) the technical nature of the adjudicative process and (2) the large volume of cases requiring determination.

The FTC illustrates pure administrative adjudication in its administration of the wool, fur, flammable fabrics, and textile acts, which require proper labeling, advertising, marketing, and so on. A large amount of the adjudicative workload of the Commission in this area is carried out through informal interpretative advice, through which potential cases are settled. In addition, as is characteristic of this type of adjudication, most existing infractions of rules are eliminated to the satisfaction of the government during the course of investigations. The accompanying table contains workload statistics of the Division of Textiles and Furs for fiscal 1960.

This table does not contain the actual number of informal cases; however, a significant proportion of those cases involving

FTC, DIVISION OF TEXTILES AND FURS—1960

1. Commercial establishments covered by industry compliance investigations	1,948
2. Products examined (sampling method)	14,673,239
3. Advertisements examined	38,005
4. Formal complaints recommended	82
5. Stipulations recommended	35
6. Matters disposed of by acceptance of discontinuance	165
7. Cases in which informal interpretative advice rendered	70,037

SOURCE: 1960 FTC Annual Report, p. 37.

informal interpretative advice represent informal case disposition, in addition to those where discontinuance of illegal practices is accepted in settlement.

As a final example of pure adjudication in the regulatory realm the ICC administers a variety of statutory provisions concerned with carrier equipment safety, including such dangerous problems as the shipment of explosive materials by rail or truck. In this area the Commission has jurisdiction over locomotive design and function, signal devices, communication systems, and the like. In 1960 the ICC noted that inspections regarding the last two, which totaled 4,495 during the year, "served to call railroad management's attention to a large number of unsatisfactory maintenance conditions for corrective action." [20] In the field of locomotive inspection the ICC conducted 108,629 locomotive examinations during 1960, from which 10 per cent were found defective in some respect. As the Commission noted, "inspection and repair reports for steam locomotives filed with district inspectors during the year totaled 14,932; for locomotives other than steam 408,366; and for multiple operated electric locomotive units, 32,-486." [21] This type of activity illustrates once again the routine but important enforcement work of a technical nature which regulatory agencies perform. It is routine because it is technical and unquestioned by the private parties concerned. Paradoxically, its very routine nature results in the strong possibility of arbitrary administrative action.

Examples of pure administrative adjudication could be multiplied at length. The FAA is involved in this area, along with the

CAB, in setting engineering standards for aircraft and airports and in securing compliance informally. The Federal Power Commission, the Food and Drug Administration, the Atomic Energy Commission, and a number of other similar federal agencies all exercise important adjudicative functions of a technical nature which preclude a meaningful formal, and in many instances even an informal, hearing.

CONCLUSION

It is evident that there is an area within the informal administrative process where almost total administrative discretion exists in adjudication. Generally this is because of the technical nature of the decisions which must be made, although other factors fortify this discretion, for instance the unusually large volume of cases and the nonadversary nature of benefit adjudication, both significant features of the pure administrative process.

Within the pure administrative process significant functions of a judicial nature have been delegated to subordinate staff. This is characteristic of the entire informal adjudicative realm. The possibility of judicial review, moreover, is entirely absent in any meaningful sense. In some instances it is excluded by law, such as in VA adjudication. In all cases decisions rest primarily upon expert, or factual, judgments which courts would be very reluctant to overrule even if they accepted review. Usually the courts have no part to play in this area of adjudication, and rarely if ever are such administrative determinations appealed to the judicial branch.

Pure administrative adjudication is characterized not only by the absence of hearings in any formal sense, but in many instances also by the elimination of informal negotiation, simply because the subject matter involved in the process of decision is not negotiable. On the other hand, in the benefit area intra-agency appellate systems have been established, as well as informal conferences at initial adjudicative levels, to afford claimants meaningful hearings on an informal basis. Even in these areas, however, a very small proportion of the total number of decisions made are challenged in any way by claimants.

The importance of the informal administrative process, of which pure administrative adjudication is a part, has been demonstrated with regard to individual rights and in terms of the total economic picture. The remaining chapter will deal with the implications of this process in terms of the traditional legal frame of reference, and with respect to recent proposals for reform made by private groups, the President, and the Congress.

Chapter VI

ADMINISTRATIVE JUSTICE AND THE INFORMAL ADMINISTRATIVE PROCESS

The stage has been set and the facts are in concerning the development and significance of informal administrative adjudication. It is evident, in view of traditional legal precepts, that administrative procedure does not conform. Although the trend in the direction of informal adjudication has been as pronounced in the judicial system as in the administrative process, it is often accepted in the former but not in the latter. Generally there is a belief, among both lawyers and administrators, that administrative law must be viewed primarily in terms of formal judicial procedure, which is to say that judicialization of the administrative process is a reality. Both groups seem to differ only as to the degree of formality present. And a great deal of confusion has developed about the real and the ideal nature of administrative law.

It is instructive to consider examples of current thinking about administrative law reform, both from the legal and from the administrative points of view. It will then be necessary to assess the validity of these current assumptions and prescriptions regarding administrative adjudication in terms of the evidence presented in this book and with respect to a model of administrative justice.

CURRENT APPROACH TO IMPROVEMENT

The historical development of legal criticism of administrative law, including common-law theory, the ABA movements of the nineteen-thirties, and the Administrative Procedure Act of 1946 has been discussed in chapter i. It was noted there that, although there are many diverse strands of thought in the ABA, an official point of view has been expressed by the organization concerning the proper role of administrative law in the legal

166

system. Current criticism continues this frame of reference. The movement for administrative law reform in the nineteen-fifties took its theme from the 1955 Hoover Commission report on legal services and procedure.[1] The Commission task force was to determine the realities of administrative adjudication, the appropriateness of the Administrative Procedure Act of 1946 in light of administrative practice, and methods for improvement. The report that was finally published emphasizes the necessity for implementing traditional legal procedure in the administrative process. To a certain extent the facts of the task-force report were incomplete, and in some instances they covered irrelevant points. The report was in excess of 400 pages, but only three or four of these were directed to the area of informal adjudication, and they indicated a fundamental misunderstanding of the nature of such adjudication in the administrative process. It is instructive to observe some of the assumptions and ideas put forth by this report as an illustration of a significant body of legal thought. A series of proposals have been introduced in Congress by the American Bar Association based upon the recommendations of the Hoover Commission and its task force.

The task force noted that there were five major policy considerations which it accepted as basic requirements of administrative procedure. First, "sound administrative procedures are indispensable to administrative justice." Justice in the administrative process "can be achieved only through law." Further, "the more closely that administrative procedures can be made to conform to judicial procedures, the greater the probability that justice will be attained in the administrative process," and in accordance with this goal "formalization of administrative procedures along judicial lines is consistent with efficiency and simplification of the administrative process. Efficiency in the administrative process has no value unless the end result is due process and fair dealing for the individual citizen. Practical formality aids efficiency by assuring that the administrative process will follow well-defined channels of authority and procedure, known to all parties, without the delays of ex parte consultation, political pressure, and improper influence." In addition, "the administrative process is improved and rendered fair and efficient by uniform standards and forms of procedure. Wide variations

in administrative procedures are confusing to the public and unnecessary to effective administrative action." [2]

In line with these basic assumptions, the task force proposed
modifications in administrative procedure through stricter statutory control and by the establishment of administrative courts
in the trade practice, labor relations, tax, and immigration fields,
with such additional courts as might be found feasible. It recommended that modifications

> should include reducing existing exemptions from statutory
> procedure, ensuring greater public information concerning
> administrative records and action, increasing public partici-
> pation in agency rule-making, conforming the administrative
> to the judicial process in agency adjudication, requiring
> greater internal separation of powers, perfecting intra-agency
> appeals, encouraging simplified procedures where feasible
> and practicable, controlling the exercise of administrative
> discretion within definitely prescribed legislative limits, and
> extending the scope of judicial review of administrative
> action which directly affects private rights.[3]

The entire report was written with undue concentration upon
formal procedure, the implication being that administrative adjudication may be conceptualized in such terms. This is not to
say that formal procedure was recommended for the informal
process, but that informal adjudication was almost completely
overlooked as a vital aspect of the total picture of administrative
law. Needless to say the tenor of the recommendations conflicts
directly with the evidence presented in this book, which indicates that administrative adjudication today is *primarily* informal, even where hearings are required by statute.

The problem that arises from reports such as that of the
Hoover Commission in 1955 is that a fundamental lack of appre-
ciation of the true nature of the administrative process leads to
inappropriate recommendations for remedy. The American Bar
Association, basing its views upon the report of the Hoover Commission, has taken up the legislative cudgels for the Commission's
proposals and recommended the establishment of administrative
courts and a stricter code of federal administrative procedure.
Although in some instances the ABA proposals differ from those

of the Hoover Commission, in general both want stricter rules of evidence to be followed than is now the practice. They also want greater independence of the hearing examiner and a closer approximation between his position and that of a judge in terms of making decisions on the basis of the facts presented by the parties during the course of the hearing. They desire less discretion on the part of the agency to overrule the examiner's decision, and the establishment of definite procedures to be followed by administrative agencies in adjudication. Such procedures would be similar to those practiced, in theory at least, by the judiciary.

With respect to the establishment of administrative courts the legal bias in some cases leads to a feeling that somehow adjudication is more respectable when carried out by an independent court which is part of the judicial branch. For this reason the Hoover Commission, and subsequently the American Bar Association, proposed that courts of original jurisdiction be established in certain well-defined areas of regulation. In addition to this, the Hoover Commission wanted to have certain functions now exercised within the administrative branch, particularly the imposition and remission of money penalties, to be transferred to the judicial branch.

The official stand of the American Bar Association conceptualizes the administrative process in terms of the legal rights and obligations of citizens. Thus, in testimony before the Senate Subcommittee on Administrative Practice and Procedure, an ABA representative noted in 1960, regarding administrative procedure, that:

A catalog of citizen complaints would include some or all of the following:

1. Judge and prosecutor: In the numerous types of disciplinary proceedings the agency is both the accuser and the judge. The agency tells the citizen "We find that you have violated this law or regulation." If the citizen disputes this, he has no choice but to give up or try to convince the agency that it was wrong in the first place.

2. Prejudgment: In proceedings where a citizen is entitled to a fair and impartial hearing, the merits of this case are frequently prejudged at the inception of the proceeding. For

example, in the issuance of a cease-and-desist order the agency has made a determination that the citizen has violated the law. Suppose, for example, a cranberry farmer was disposed to contest the merits of the Government's action last year in condemning his crop, the only tribunal before which he could get a hearing on this dispute would be before the very same officials who ordered the condemnation. Pause for a moment to reflect on what a rude shock this is to a citizen who has been taught that he is entitled to justice and a fair and impartial hearing. In agency litigation the citizen frequently has the impression that his case was decided before, not after, the hearing.

3. Prior identification with case: It is customary for a judge to disqualify himself from sitting in any case with which he has had any previous association. This is considered essential to an impartial judgment on the evidence in the record. In the agency environment more frequently than not the agency members have some prior identification with the proceeding, which the citizen litigant may consider to his disadvantage. But there is no practice of agency member disqualification by reason of prior identification with a case. . . .

4. Judge and litigant: In many agency proceedings the agency is acting both as litigant and as a judge. In its capacity as litigant the agency and the citizen are opposing parties, and the citizen's controversy is going to be decided by his opposing litigant—the agency. . . .[4]

In addition to these traditional criticisms, which remind one of ABA statements during the 'thirties, the ABA wants more hearing examiner authority, decisions to be made on the record, complete judicial review, and so on.[5] In other words, in 1963, as in 1933, the ABA and some groups in the legal profession seem to be pushing for complete formalization of the administrative process in terms of internal agency procedure, and in some instances legal opinion favors administrative courts which presumably would solve procedural problems by entirely removing the function of adjudication from the hands of administrative agencies.

Current Administrative Approach to Improvement

At the present time the administrative process is being sub-jected to harsh criticism from administratively oriented groups, mostly lawyers, as well as from official ABA representatives. A member of the Civil Aeronautics Board stirred up the adminis-trative branch when he resigned in disgust in September, 1959, and sent a long memorandum to the President outlining what he considered to be the major problems of regulatory adminis-tration. After this point, the individual involved, Louis J. Hector, became the spokesman for a significant school of thought re-garding administrative reorganization. Typically, he concentrated upon what is generally considered to be the top echelon of ad-ministration, which undoubtedly makes his recommendations of limited validity. As will be emphasized, it is evident that the most significant quantitative, and probably qualitative, adjudica-tion is often performed at the subordinate staff level within the administrative process. In any event, Hector agreed with the ABA that separate judicial bodies should be created to handle major regulatory cases. Like the President's Committee on Ad-ministrative Management (1937) before him, he proposed ideally the abolition of the independent regulatory agency.

My own solution for the problems of these agencies would be to transfer to the executive branch of the Government all administrative policy-making and rule-making duties of the agencies; to transfer to a special court the responsibility for deciding *major litigated regulatory cases;* and to transfer to the Department of Justice the functions of investigating and prosecuting now performed by the agencies. It is my belief that this would give greater control over regulatory opera-tions to both Congress and the executive; that it would get the regulatory job done far more effectively; and that it would give a fuller measure of judicial process to the liti-gants in major contested cases.[6]

Hector reflects the general administrative concern with policy-making; he seems willing to leave adjudication, which he defines narrowly, to some outside group. To him, one of the major reasons for transferring the adjudicative function is to relieve regulatory commissioners from the burden of having to decide a large volume of cases; they would thus be freer to devote their time to policy formulation, which is of overriding significance. He abhors the ABA's attempts to judicialize administrative proceedings presently performed by the agencies. Again, he reflects a typical administrative feeling when he states:

> There is a vast amount of necessary regulatory activity which simply will not fit into any judicial scheme, either because it is so detailed and voluminous that it can only be handled administratively or because it involves so many conflicting interests and policies that it can be handled only by prolonged informal conferences, exchanges of views, and directed staff work.
>
> The only way to judicialize the work of the agencies is to turn them into courts and make them act in all matters like courts. If this were done, we would merely substitute one set of problems for another.
>
> . . . No one can tell you how to speed up the work of the agencies as they are presently constituted and at the same time further formalize and judicialize their procedures. . . .
>
> Whatever it is called—"judicial standards" or "redtape"— formal procedural complexity is an essential element in judicial process and the agencies, in their present organizational form, cannot stand any more of it. Unless their judicial and executive functions are completely separated, any attempt at further judicializing the work of the agencies will either increase the already broad gap between theory and practice or further increase the already intolerable delays.[7]

The problem of the separation of policy-making from adjudication forms a key part of current administrative proposals for reform. Although hearing examiners are separated from appointed officials, both play an important part in policy formulation; the result is that a hearing examiner, on the basis of independent judgment after a hearing, may arrive at a conclusion with profound policy implications, but one which is nevertheless completely at odds with *agency* policy. To illustrate this point Hector noted, with regard to one CAB case, that

The hearing examiner who heard the *Seven States* case did not know what the Board had in mind in terms of extent of service.

The Board had in its own thinking come around to the conclusion that any town which had any reasonable chance of producing 5 passengers a day should have a chance to see if it could do so, and if it could then it should have an airline.

The hearing examiner did not know this, because he is independent, and the Board could not talk to him.

So he spent 2 years hearing evidence and turning out a 500-odd page opinion.

It came up to the Board, and the Board's first reaction was, "This wasn't what we had in mind at all. We were thinking of a much more extensive route pattern."

Certainly if the Board could have told this hearing examiner in the beginning what they had in mind and then could have checked back with him as he went along and was drawing up his plan the whole thing would have proceeded much faster. Certainly General Eisenhower, when he was planning the invasion of France did not turn it over to the staff and then not talk to them again until the plan was all finished.

But this is the way that the Board handles these big policy cases. They just throw the naked question at the hearing examiner, and then don't talk to him until he is all through. As a result he does not know what they have in mind, and a large proportion of the time they reverse him on policy grounds.

If this could be done on an informal interchange staff basis it could be done far more promptly. But then when you have got to pick the carriers to fly the routes, I think you need a full judicial trial.[8]

Here the administrator is objecting to the independence of the hearing examiner, claiming that his supposed "judicial" functions are really "policy-making."

A number of management surveys carried out under the auspices of the Bureau of the Budget by private management firms, between 1953 and 1960, confirmed some of Hector's views, and emphasized not only that further judicialization would be undesirable, but also that within the administrative process there is too great reliance upon formal procedure at the present time. This is particularly interesting, in the light of the evidence presented in this book concerning the extent of informal adjudication. Nevertheless, these surveys concluded:

The effectiveness of the agencies in regulating sectors of economic activity in accordance with the social and economic goals set by the Congress is greatly influenced by the scope and extent of judicial procedure. Much of the activities of the agencies now is carried out through the laborious and time-consuming processes associated with the courtroom. As a result, large backlogs of cases accumulate, and agency decisions are delayed for months, often for years. The industries being regulated are unable to make long-range planning decisions, particularly in technological growth areas, because of the regulatory lag. Delays and backlogs have meant denial of justice in some cases and economic losses in others. . . .

In the judgment of many observers the trend toward formal procedure has gone too far in recent years and should be reversed. Many feel that too little use is made of informal processes for rule-making and other decisions not required to be made on the record where the essential character of the issue is public interest rather than private right.

The appropriateness of using formal hearings to obtain from all interested parties the necessary facts for some types of regulatory decisions is questioned. Modern fact-gathering and data-processing techniques could provide better information more quickly and at less cost, and would greatly reduce the scope and length of the formal hearing.

Formal procedures also make it extremely difficult for hearing examiners to obtain the assistance of staff experts in conducting hearings and reaching decisions on the complex economic and social issues involved in certain kinds of regulatory cases. Single individuals, usually with legal training, are expected to rule on questions of relevance of evidence and to provide a penetrating analysis of all facets of presentations made to them by what are, in many major cases, balanced teams of experts.

Hearing records are voluminous, unwieldy, and difficult to analyze. Because of the emphasis on assuring every interested party a hearing, the necessity for deciding the case on the record, the lack of preparation of examiners prior to the hearing, failure to exploit pre-hearing conferences, the examiners' uncertainty about board standards for deciding cases, and the dilatory tactics of litigants in some cases, voluminous and sometimes irrelevant testimony is permitted. At the same time, because of the adversary approach, the voluminous record does not contain all the essential information required for a rational decision. The size of the record is a serious handicap, not only to the hearing examiners, but also to the boards and the courts in reviewing cases on appeal.[9]

The Landis Report—1960

The Landis Report, written for President Kennedy, dealt with the problems of regulatory agencies, as has been characteristic of most reports on these agencies, in terms of top management and major cases. The report reflected the administrative views discussed above. It was primarily concerned with policy-making, although no attempt was made to emphasize the distinction between adjudication and policy formulation. The regulatory process, as exemplified by the independent agencies, was considered unified, although Landis did in several instances indicate that different procedures should be employed in certain kinds of cases because of their adjudicative, rather than rule-making, nature.

At the beginning of the report the major problems of regulatory administration are related in terms of: (1) delays in the disposition of adjudicative proceedings; (2) excessive costs of administrative proceedings generally; (3) lack of high caliber personnel; (4) prevalence of unethical conduct, particularly in terms of ex parte representation; (5) inefficient procedure, particularly as a result of excessive "judicialization"; (6) inadequate organizational structures, causing a lack of unified policy direction within and between agencies; (7) lack of effective presidential control over major regulatory policies.[10]

Various remedies were proposed by Landis to cope with these problems. He recommended presidential appointment of chairmen, where this power does not exist, to provide greater over-all coördination of regulatory policy. The President would be aided in this task by the establishment of a special office to deal with such agencies within the Executive Office of the President. Internal efficiency of the agencies would be strengthened through an increase in the power of the chairmen, and through the delegation of formal adjudicative functions to hearing examiners, in order to eliminate the necessity of agency review. In this way more unified direction would be given to the agencies, and the top echelon would have greater time to devote to policy formulation. Landis recommended a greater emphasis upon informal adjudicative techniques within the formal stage of adjudication, that is, by hearing examiners. He admired the success of informal adjudication in such agencies as the National Labor Relations Board; however, he did not note in particular the vast use of this method of settlement throughout the administrative process. He hinted that perhaps the administrative process was too judicialized. Finally, he proposed measures to obtain high-caliber personnel, measures such as longer terms of office, more prestige to the chairmen of agencies, and the like. Many of Landis's proposals were incorporated into legislative bills; however, the bulk of the legislative proposals were turned down because of agency and outside interest opposition. Further, Congress considers these agencies as arms of the legislative branch; therefore, it is not desirous of increasing presidential control over them any more than is absolutely necessary. With the exception of an increase in the power of the chairmen of some agencies (the CAB in particular) and greater *de jure* delegation of adjudicative power to trial examiners, the agencies remain unaffected by the attempts of Landis and President Kennedy to reorganize their structures and streamline their procedures.

Summary

Present-day criticism of the independent regulatory agencies by the American Bar Association and some of its representatives concentrates upon administrative incapacity to protect the rights of private parties in administrative proceedings through proper use of formal judicial techniques. Criticism from the administrative standpoint, on the other hand, focuses upon the importance of proper *policy* formulation and coördination, and upon the need for greater efficiency in handling the adjudicative and legislative tasks of the agencies. The orientation of each group is reflected in their respective proposals for administrative law reform. While reforms are proposed in rapid fire fashion, the agencies in the meantime rely upon their political strength to maintain positions of autonomy. In this the stronger agencies, politically speaking, prevail over any attempts at reorganization, while the weaker ones are reformed, albeit mildly, by Congress and the President.

EVALUATION OF REFORM PROPOSALS

An observer, viewing the numerous recommendations for improvement of administrative procedure, can only be confused, for the practical and theoretical motivations of reformers differ. Each group seeking change views the administrative process in terms of one aspect of its operation; thus, the official viewpoint of the American Bar Association is based above all on the need to protect the rights of private parties in administrative proceedings, while administrative-minded reformers seek to increase efficiency.

When dealing with the independent regulatory agencies and others exercising significant power to affect the rights and obligations of individuals, the administrative functions of particular concern are (1) rule-making and (2) adjudication. The rule-making function involves substantive and procedural policy formulation. The former concerns over-all agency policy regarding economic regulation of a particular industry or interpretation of law as it pertains to individual rights, as in the operation of the Internal Revenue Service, the Veterans Administration, and the like. The latter aspect of rule-making pertains to the formulation of procedural regulations by which the agency will enforce substantive policy. Theoretically, once general agency policy has been established, conflicts between such policy and private action must be adjudicated, that is, the agency cannot enforce its will by fiat. Lest one think this is self-evident, it must be stated that completely arbitrary administrative action in enforcement is prevented legally only by statutory and constitutional limitation, with the former being more important than the latter in most areas of administrative action. After all, Congress controls the appellate jurisdiction of the courts and is able to curtail the power of the judicial branch over administrative agencies. In most fields this can be done without upsetting constitutional norms established by the courts themselves; hence, the possibility of strong judicial opposition to limitations on their power is generally absent.[11] The function of administrative adjudication pertains to agency determination of the rights and obligations of private parties in terms of agency rules based upon statutory law. It may be distinguished from rule-making on the basis of its specific application relative to the general nature of agency formulation of rules (policy) which apply across the board to designated industry groups and individuals. It is evident that the functions of administrative agencies are highly complex. Within each agency various duties are performed which differ in nature and object; at the same time, these seemingly different functions complement each other.

In order to evaluate potential changes in administrative procedure numerous factors must be considered and related. First, the position of such agencies within the political and constitutional system must be recognized. This includes the relationships between such agencies and Congress, the President, and the judicial branch. In addition, politically speaking, the role of agencies, acting as interest groups, as well as their interaction with outside groups, is relevant. The Constitution initially shapes the context of agency action, and extra-constitutional factors complete the picture. Both theoretical and practical considerations have to be taken into account. Proposals which do not conform to this context may be irrelevant because of their inconsistency with the norms of the system; thus, such proposals might be theoretically and practically invalid.

Apart from a general determination of the context of administrative action, in the area of administrative adjudication with which this book deals a model must be outlined which delineates criteria of administrative justice, consistent with the political and constitutional context, against which present procedure may be measured. In particular it will be necessary to contrast the relative efficacy of informal, in terms of such criteria, as opposed to formal administrative adjudication.

The Political and Constitutional Context of Administrative Action

The most important part of the Constitution which determines the general position of the administrative branch within the governmental system is the separation of powers. Here lies the unchangeable root of many of the most criticized aspects of administrative behavior. No provision was made in the Constitution for a "fourth branch," and constitutional terminology is vague enough to leave the position of the administrative process within the scheme of government ambiguous. All three primary branches of the government have constitutional justification for controlling various aspects of administrative operation and organization. The Constitution, by dividing power among the three major departments, eliminated the possibility of establishing one focal point of control over administrative activity. Two immediate consequences arise from this fact: (1) the three departments of government, but particularly the executive and legislative branches, fight among themselves to control administrative agencies and thus increase their own power; (2) the agencies, because of the lack of unified control, can in many instances exercise autonomous power. The latter situation is fortified by other considerations, such as administrative control over information (*expertise*) flowing to the legislature and in many cases to the President, outside political support, propaganda activities, and the like. The Constitution gives each major branch of the government both the *means* and the *motives* to resist encroachment from coördinate departments; hence, conflict is built into the Constitution. Each of the three branches considers itself independent, to a certain degree, as was intended. Differing presidential and congressional constituencies provide the principal basis for antagonistic attitudes, although other constitutional provisions, such as the different terms of office in each branch of the legislature and the Presidency, fortify this antagonism. It is not in the interest of Congress to strengthen the Presidency; therefore, when administrative agencies are created or reorganized congressional tendency is to place them outside of presidential purview, insofar as is feasible.

In addition to constitutional factors lessening presidential control over administrative agencies, outside interest groups and the agencies themselves (once established) pressure Congress to maintain their independence. Several points should be noted in this respect. First, outside interest groups generally find access easier to statutorily independent (as opposed to dependent) agencies, although there are many agencies within the executive branch that are as closely related to outside interest groups as the independent agencies. This is related to the fact that all agencies wish to maintain a balance of political support over opposition, and they will usually turn to those groups that can provide such support. If they are independent they must rely upon Congress to a greater extent for appropriations and other items necessary for effective operation and continuity. Congress, at the same time, is greatly influenced by powerful private interest groups, who generally have considerable power to make or break a regulatory agency. For many agencies the most effective basis of political support is provided by the very interests they regulate, and if they become antagonistic to such groups they may run into trouble over appropriations, appointments, and the like in Congress.[12] Of course many agencies without strong clientele groups may find a valuable source of political support in the Presidency; consequently, his control over this portion of the administrative process is strengthened politically.

The administrative process, then, fits into the constitutional scheme of separation of powers in an ambiguous fashion. It is evident that the primary purpose of the framers was to avoid too great concentration of political power in the hands of one department; thus, the inability of any department to control the agencies completely is not inconsistent with constitutional purpose.

The judicial system plays its part in controlling administrative procedure (and sometimes policy-making) through judicial review. This concept was not originally part of the Constitution; however, it fits into constitutional and common-law doctrine as evolved through custom and usage. In addition, as indicated in the first chapter, judicial review of administrative determinations is an essential part of common-law theory. Thus the legitimacy of the theory of judicial review forms another necessary part of the context of administrative action; however, in reality judicial review has been strictly limited by congressional laws as well as by the application of judicial self-restraint. The Administrative Procedure Act of 1946 recognizes the importance of judicial review and expands its scope; at the same time it does not interfere with statutory preclusion of review or limitation upon agency procedure. The courts themselves have been reluctant to review expert administrative determinations and generally will not consider agency decisions made within the bounds of statutory discretion.

It is clear that the institutional context of administrative action indicates the existence of an administrative process which is semi-autonomous. As noted above, the functions of the agencies also lead to freedom of action in most areas, for their work is characterized by high volume and *expertise*, which precludes much outside interference. Their organizational structures are characterized by size, complexity, specialization, and in many instances the existence of extensive field staffs. Both the organizational and functional characteristics of the agencies lead to internal delegation of power as well as to isolation from the outside.

In summary, constitutional, political, and functional characteristics of the administrative process lead to a significant amount of autonomy in operation. Perhaps paradoxically, this seems to conform to the norms of the American governmental system, for the administrative branch takes its place among coördinate departments to form a fourth branch of the government which to a degree controls and interferes with the operations of the other departments and at the same time is subject to certain outside checks. It has evolved to become part of the "checks and balances" mechanism. And administrative agencies, in addition to adding this new dimension to the constitutional scheme, conform to democratic norms in that they function as interest groups in a society which supports pluralism, channeling the power of private groups into public policy. In fact, the way these agencies act conforms to both constitutional and democratic theory. The position of the administrative branch cannot readily be changed, because it stems from basic constitutional provisions and political norms.

Criteria for Administrative Adjudication

It is evident that criteria for administrative adjudication must be realistic, in terms of the institutional and functional context of administrative action. This is not to say that the status quo must be supported inevitably; however, the basic reasons for the establishment of the present system must be recognized, as indicated above, and if a change is to be made in the operation and organization of agencies those conditions presently existing which shape the status quo must be changed.

From an institutional point of view, administrative adjudication was *purposely* placed in the hands of the same agency charged with the formulation of policy. This was done by Congress because of general judicial hostility to legislative purpose in regulatory fields, also because the function of adjudication was recognized as a valuable adjunct to policy enforcement. The thrust of original regulatory statutes was in the direction of vigorous policy enforcement in the public interest, which was to be defined by the agencies themselves. Once such an institutional context is established it is difficult to change, because various interest groups, including the agencies themselves, learn to work within the system to gain advantage. This desire to keep things as they are is fortified by the constitutional and political factors noted above.

From a functional point of view it is clearly necessary to balance the requirements of policy formulation with the needs of proper individual adjudication. The fact is that the bulk of administrative adjudication is carried out at an informal level;

therefore, recommendations dealing with the top level cover the field only to a very limited extent. Regardless of whether or not a separation is made at the top level between supposed policy-making and adjudication, a combination of functions will remain at the informal level. Should such a system be changed through greater formalization of the administrative process? Or can informal adjudication fit into a legitimate scheme of administrative law and meet the requirements of administrative justice?

It is possible, in analyzing the requirements of administrative law, to construct a model which will delineate the criteria of administrative justice. This is necessary in order to contrast formal and informal procedure. To begin with, the British concept of "natural justice" may be used, for it essentially coincides with broad criteria of due process of law and is consistent with basic common-law theory, although it may differ in some respects. In the famous Report of the Committee on Ministers' Powers this concept was developed and applied to administrative law in Great Britain.[13] The Committee notes with respect to the tenets of natural justice that "it is beyond doubt that there are certain canons of judicial conduct to which all tribunals and persons who have to give judicial or quasi-judicial decisions ought to conform. The principles on which they rest are . . . implicit in the rule of law." [14]

The first principle of natural justice is that a man cannot be judge in his own cause. Disqualifying bias is difficult to define; however, a minimum requirement is that an official ought not have a direct *personal* interest in the outcome of a case which he is to judge. The Committee on Ministers' Powers felt that bias as to public policy should constitute disqualification; however, American administrative law makes a distinction between a personal and policy bias, tending to support disqualification in the former situation but not in the latter. A reasonable policy bias does not result in disqualification, but no official should be permitted to adjudicate a case in which he *might* have a personal interest. Presumably, a policy bias can be changed if the evidence presented during a hearing (formal or informal) is convincing enough; however, a personal bias is irrational with regard to the factual context, and can result normally in only one judgment which favors the interests of the biased adjudicator. The basis of policy bias is rational consideration of the facts, whereas a personal bias stems from self-interest. A policy bias can be overcome, a personal bias cannot.

The second principle of natural justice has two phases. In the words of the Committee:

> No party ought to be condemned unheard; and if his right to be heard is to be a reality, he must know in good time the case which he has to meet. But on neither branch of this principle can any particular procedure (i) by which the party is informed of the case which he has to meet, or (ii) by which the evidence and argument are "heard" be regarded as fundamental. That a Minister or a Ministerial Tribunal does not conform to the procedure of the Courts in either respect imports no disregard of natural justice. There is, for instance, no natural right to an oral hearing.[15]

The committee advanced two further corollary principles of natural justice: (1) parties must know the reason for the decision made in their case; (2) parties must know the nature of any material or recommendations made at an initial administrative level which is taken into account by officials authorized to render a final decision. The latter concept raises the problem of institutional decision-making, which is of considerable concern in American administrative law.

The criteria of natural justice are not adequate by themselves to provide standards of administrative procedure. Three additional components of a model for administrative justice must be noted: (1) the need for an opportunity for review of administrative decisions; (2) the need for accurate fact-finding; (3) the need for *policy* considerations to be taken into account properly in the process of exercising judicial functions. Ideally, under the terms of traditional common-law theory, *judicial* review must be maintained over administrative adjudication. The possibility of such review should be open, even if rarely used, for a system to be in accordance with common-law doctrine; however, it may be questioned whether review must always be by courts. A sense of fairness may be maintained if review exists within the administrative agency concerned, or within the administrative branch. Further, in this respect, issues involving *expertise* may be better resolved by specialists familiar with agency operation. From the agency's point of view, policy considerations will be given more understanding treatment within an administrative appellate system than in the judicial branch.

A second important need for administrative justice to be realized is accurate fact-finding. Machinery must exist for proper determination of facts in any given case. This is the principal function of common-law procedural rules, and a vital need in any type of adjudication; however, the types of cases and characteristics of personnel differ markedly in the administrative process relative to the common-law realm. Insofar as juries are used in common-law cases, adjudication depends upon personnel with less continuity of service and less *expertise* than found in the administrative process. The judge may counterbalance this lack on the part of juries to some extent; however, the basic distinction remains. With regard to the type of case handled by administrative agencies it is doubtful that the formal testimonial process of proof, designed to keep irrelevancies and prejudicial matter away from juries and to gain the advantage of demeanor evidence, is as efficacious to administrative justice as it is in a normal case tried in a common-law court. Administrative fact-finding must depend to a large extent upon independent investigation accomplished through an institutional decision-making process in which experts participate. Demeanor evidence is of little importance in administrative proceedings, and such techniques as cross-examination are often cumbersome in attempting to arrive at expert determinations. Efficient fact-finding requires flexibility and the utilization of modern research techniques which cannot be used within the framework of traditional common-law doctrine.

A final component for a model of administrative justice is the existence of a proper relationship between policy and adjudication. Administrative determinations must be made not only in accordance with facts presented during the course of a hearing, but also in terms of policy considerations. The agency involved in adjudication must roam beyond the boundaries which would normally be set by strict adherence to judicial procedure and take official notice of circumstances bearing upon policy interests defined by statute or administrative rules and directives. In line with its policy function, the agency must be able and willing to seize the initiative and take necessary corrective action when required. The umpire theory of law cannot operate effectively in the modern regulatory realm.

The problem of formulating a valid relationship between policy and adjudication is perhaps the most complex in administrative law. Those who would separate completely adjudicative functions into administrative courts, leaving the enforcement arms of agencies dangling separately or merged into executive departments, overlook the intimate relationship that exists between the two functions. Anyone making a judicial determination involving economic regulation, benefit programs, tax measures, and so on must, in the final analysis, have a clear conception of governing rules or policy. Such adjudicative decisions cannot be made in a policy vacuum; therefore, by substituting one group for another engaged in adjudication, to a substantial degree policy power is also transferred to the new group. As the old saying goes, "It is those who interpret the law that count, not those that formulate the general rules." This is not to say in any way that ideally the same group within an agency that brings a case should also adjudicate it. Quite clearly, this lessens the chance that the private party involved will receive a fair and objective judgment; but, although it is possible to separate functions of prosecution and adjudication within the same agency at the hearing examiner level, at the lower levels where most informal adjudication takes place such separation cannot realistically be achieved. Because of this latter fact, and because it is extremely difficult to determine exactly what constitutes adjudication and what is policy-formulation, the extent and permanence of informal adjudication should be recognized, and an effort should be made to maintain procedures at that level consistent with criteria of administrative justice.

Formal and Informal Procedure Evaluated

To what extent does informal adjudication, as presently functioning, conform to the criteria of administrative justice delineated above, and what is its relative efficacy in this respect when compared to formal adjudication? First, there is little doubt that formal adjudication, with requirements for adequate notice and apprisal, hearing with cross-examination, right to counsel, a decision on the record, and opportunity for review, meets the standards of natural justice which comprise the first part of the model of administrative justice. In the formal area (that is, where formal adjudication is required by statute or, in rare instances, by constitutional due process), the Administrative Procedure Act applies and aids directly in implementing the standards of natural justice.[16] Except in rare instances, appeal may be taken from formal decisions to a court of law, provided the necessary legal requirements have been fulfilled and the court accepts review. Standards of natural justice may not be as adequately fulfilled in the formal administrative process as in a court of law; however, relative to the informal adjudicative realm, criteria of natural justice are followed more consistently and with more predictability in the formal realm.

In the informal area, on the other hand, it is largely within the discretion of the agency and the administrator involved whether or not strict standards of due process and natural justice will be followed. It is important to point out that due process does not require formal procedure; but due process is more likely to be followed where such procedure is operative. It is quite possible, on the other hand, that a sense of fairness may be present in the informal adjudicative area which would fulfill the requirements of natural justice and due process of law. This *possibility*, and in many instances it is a probability, is of considerable importance because informal procedure, which does not fulfill criteria of natural justice as adequately as formal procedure, nor provide for review as adequately (from the standpoint of the private party) as that performed by the judicial branch, does provide more appropriate machinery for fact-finding and greater flexibility for taking into account policy considerations than the approach of formal adjudication.

The *raison d'être* of the administrative process is the increasing need for more flexibility than is provided by either Congress or the courts. Modern regulation requires specialization, *expertise*, continuity of service, and flexibility for utilization of a variety of skills which would not be possible operating within a strict common-law framework. Even the formal administrative process was intended to be more flexible than a court of law, and the courts

have permitted this utilization of more flexible procedure; however, it is actually the informal administrative process that
epitomizes those characteristics for which there was a felt need
at the time of the creation of the administrative agency as a
regulatory device. Informal procedure offers the best possibility
of effective use of a combination of techniques in the regulatory
realm; thus informal investigation through an institutional process
is the most effective way in which to ascertain relevant facts pertaining to many situations that often confront administrative
agencies, and policy considerations may shape the final decision
insofar as necessary for the protection of the public interest,
convenience, or necessity.

In contrasting the fact-finding possibilities of the administrative as opposed to the judicial (formal) process Landis has
noted:

> The test of the judicial process, traditionally, is not the fair
> disposition of the controversy; it is the fair disposition of
> the *controversy upon the record as made by the parties.* True,
> there are collateral sources of information which often affect
> judicial determinations. There is the more or less limited
> discretion under the doctrine of judicial notice; and there is
> the inarticulated but nonetheless substantial power to choose
> between competing premises based upon off-the-record con-
> siderations. But, in strictness, the judge must not know of
> the events of the controversy except as these may have been
> presented to him, in due form, by the parties. . . . Nor is he
> permitted to conduct an investigation to determine what
> policy is best adapted to the demands of time and place,
> even though he is aware that sooner or later he will be con-
> fronted with the necessity, through the processes of judicial
> decision, of shaping policy in that particular field.[17]

On the other hand, in order for the administrative process to be
successful "it is imperative that controversies be decided as
'rightly' as possible, independently of the formal record the
parties themselves produce. The ultimate test of the administrative [process] is the policy that it formulates; not the fairness as
between the parties of the disposition of a controversy on a
record of their own making." [18] The underlying assumption of
formal adjudication in accordance with common-law criteria is

that all the relevant facts of a particular case will be produced through an adversary process; however, this is not the case in administrative law where relevant "facts" are gained from a broad and complex area, and where in addition a case cannot by statutory law be disposed of purely on the basis of such facts. Policy, in terms of the "public interest," must be taken into account.

With this in mind it is possible to conclude that administrative adjudication meets the requirements of administrative justice, which must be viewed from both the individual's and the government's point of view, most consistently through utilization of flexible, informal procedure. This is primarily because fact-finding and public policy needs can be more easily met through informal adjudication, which can at the same time develop a sense of fairness consistent with natural justice.

Current Reform Proposals Evaluated

It is submitted that current ABA and administrative proposals for procedural reform are theoretically not valid, and that they are unrealistic in terms of the context of administrative action. The recommendations for greater formalization of administrative procedure are inconsistent with the theoretical model developed above. It is also doubtful that such formalization could be meaningful in terms of the present functional context of administrative action, for the fact is that most adjudication is handled at the informal level, before any formal process is reached. This is because such settlement procedure is accepted by both the government and the private parties concerned. As has been noted many times, there are powerful sanctions, informal and automatic, as well as other factors, which preclude formal proceedings in many cases of administrative adjudication. In terms of the total picture of administrative law, moreover, reorganizations and procedural changes at the top level will not affect appreciably the lower staff levels; these will continue to function on an informal basis, with the consent of the parties within their jurisdiction.

Administrative proposals for greater efficiency, a separation of judicial and policy-making functions in some instances, and greater presidential control, also are out of line with the constitutional and political context; at the same time they ignore the vitality of informal adjudication. Constitutional and political factors point to a continuance of a semi-autonomous administrative branch, which in a way adds a fourth dimension to the traditional tripartite separation-of-powers scheme of government.

CONCLUSION

This book has attempted to describe and analyze the significance of the informal administrative process of adjudication. The area is in the twilight zone, and generally has not been appreciated by many concerned with the development of administrative law. A semi-autonomous administrative branch has been postulated, and this will undoubtedly stir up loud protests among those who feel that control from the outside is an absolutely necessary part of any bureaucratic system. It has been submitted, however, that in fact the administrative branch adds a new dimension to the separation of powers scheme, which was predicated on the belief that no branch of government should be controlled to any substantial degree by coördinate branches.

On the other hand it has not been stated that informal administrative adjudication must be maintained exactly as it is, but simply that its vital role must be recognized and dealt with in a realistic fashion. It cannot be abolished, but it can be brought into conformity with concepts of natural justice and the needs of public policy formulation in the public interest. To ignore informal adjudication is to overlook the very basis of administrative law today. To recognize its significance is to take an important step in the direction of a realistic and theoretically valid appraisal of the requirements of the government and the needs of the individual in the administrative process.

Notes

INTRODUCTION: Pp. 1–3

[1] This question will be further investigated from a legal point of view, *below*.

[2] John Dickinson, *Administrative Justice and the Supremacy of Law* (Cambridge: Harvard University Press, 1927), p. 21.

CHAPTER I: Pp. 5–30

[1] Constitution of the United States, Art. III, § 1.

[2] *ICC.* v. *Brimson*, 154 U.S. 447 (1894); *In re Sanborn*, 148 U.S. 222 (1893); *U.S.* v. *Ferreira*, 13 How. 40, 48 (1852); *American Insurance Co.* v. *Canter*, 1 Pet. 511 (1828); *Hayburn's Case*, 2 Dall. 409 410 (1792).

[3] *Prentis* v. *Atlantic Coast Line*, 211 U.S. 210 (1908); *Dreyer* v. *Illinois*, 187 U.S. 71, 83, 84 (1902).

[4] *Murray* v. *Hoboken Land & Improvement Co.*, 18 How. 272, 284 (1856).

[5] Westel W. Willoughby, *The Constitutional Law of the United States* (New York: Baker, Voorhis, 1910), II, 1277. For further discussion see 1 Davis, *Admin. Law Treatise* § 1.09 (1958).

[6] 4 *Institutes* 71.

[7] A. V. Dicey, *Introduction to the Study of the Law of the Constitution* (8th ed., London: MacMillan & Co., 1915), pp. 183–184.

[8] *Ibid.*, p. 189. For discussion relevant to this area see 1 Davis, *Admin. Law Treatise* § 1.08 (1958).

[9] Dicey, *op. cit.* note 7, p. 191.

[10] *Ibid.*, p. 192.

[11] A. V. Dicey, "The Development of Administrative Law in England," 31 *Law Quarterly Review* 148 (1915).

[12] Dicey, *Law of the Constitution*, op. cit. note 7, pp. 38–39. Emphasis added.

[13] Roscoe Pound, "Justice According to Law," 14 *Col. L. Rev.* 1, at 18 (1914).

[14] *Ibid.*, p. 14. Emphasis added.

[15] *Ibid.*, pp. 21–22.

[16] *Ibid.*, p. 24.

[17] *Ibid.*, p. 25.

[18] Roscoe Pound, "Justice According to Law," (Part III); 14 *Columbia Law Review* 103, at 108 (1914).

[19] *Ibid.*, p. 108

[20] Roscoe Pound, *The Spirit of the Common Law* (Boston: Marshall Jones Co., 1921).

[21] *Ibid.*, p. 1.

[22] *Ibid.*, p. 2.

[23] *Ibid.*, pp. 72–73.

[24] *Ibid.*, p. 73. Emphasis supplied.

[25] *Ibid.*, p. 74.
[26] *Ibid.*, p. 80.
[27] *Ibid.*, p. 183. For further discussion of legal opposition to administrative law see 1 Davis, *Admin. Law Treatise,* § 1.06–1.07 (1958).
[28] John Dickinson, *Administrative Justice and the Supremacy of Law* (Cambridge: Harvard University Press, 1927), pp. 36–37.
[29] *Ibid.*, pp. 37–38. See 1 Davis, *Admin. Law Treatise,* § 1.08 (1958), for a critique of Dickinson.
[30] 58 *ABA Rept.* 410–411 (1933). Emphasis added. Note also 1 Davis, *Admin. Law Treatise,* § 1.04–1.05 (1958).
[31] 59 *ABA Rept.* 539–564 (1934).
[32] See 61 *ABA Rept.* 221, 225, 234 (1936) for indications of opposition to the administrative court proposal.
[33] For the text of both the ABA bill and the Walter-Logan bill see U.S., House, Subcommittee No. 4 of the Committee on the Judiciary, *Administrative Law,* Hearings, 76th Cong., 1st sess. (1939), p. 119.
[34] § 2(a). For the text of the bill see *Ibid.*
[35] Administrative Procedure Act of 1946 (hereinafter cited as APA). 60 Stat. 237, §§ 3, 5, 7, 8.
[36] APA § 10.
[37] See, for example, *Ramspect* v. *Federal Trial Examiners Conference,* 345 U.S. 128 (1953). Note also 2 Davis, *Admin. Law Treatise,* §§ 10.01–10.06 (1958).
[38] *NBC* v. *FCC,* 132 F.2d, 545, 560 (1942).
[39] Of course early common-law procedures, such as ordeal and battle, were dropped as later essentials to due process.
[40] *Weimer* v. *Bunbury,* 30 Mich. 201, 211 (1874). See also 1 Davis, *Admin. Law Treatise,* §§ 7.01–7.20 (1958).
[41] 227 U.S. 88 (1913).
[42] *Ibid.*, at 91. In the instant case a statutory provision was involved requiring a hearing; however, the problem was not that a hearing was not given but that it was inadequate. Further, the language of the Court generalizes the proposition that administrative judgments determining rights require a proper hearing in order to conform to standards of due process.
[43] 290 U.S. 190 (1933).
[44] *Ibid.*, at 199.
[45] 86 Cong. Rec. 13942 (1940).
[46] Attorney General's Committee on Administrative Procedure, *Final Report,* S. Doc. No. 8, 77th Cong., 1st Sess., 1941: p. 35.
[47] *Ibid.*, p. 5.
[48] 1887 ICC Annual Rept., p. 26.
[49] 1901 ICC Annual Rept., p. 17.
[50] 1907 ICC Annual Rept., p. 120.
[51] 1887 ICC Annual Rept., pp. 27–28.

CHAPTER II: Pp. 31–61

[1] Bernard Schwartz, "Procedural Due Process in Federal Administrative Law," 25 *N.Y.U.L. Rev.* 553–554 (1950). See 1 Davis, *Admin. Law Treatise* §§ 7.01–7.20 (1958) for a discussion of this entire area.
[2] One need go no further than the APA of 1946 to illustrate this point.
[3] 239 U.S. 441 (1915).

⁴ *Ibid.*, at 443.

⁵ *Ibid.*, at 445.

⁶ 210 U.S. 373 (1908).

⁷ 274 U.S. 564 (1927).

⁸ *Ibid.*, at 583.

⁹ Rate-making is generally considered a legislative function; however, the specific nature of the application of many rates makes the designation of such rate-making as adjudication appropriate.

¹⁰ *Chicago, M. & St. P. Railway Co.* v. *Minnesota*, 134 U.S. 418 (1890); *Norwegian Nitrogen Products Co.* v. *U.S.*, 288 U.S. 294 (1933); *Jordan* v. *American Eagle Fire Ins. Co.*, 169 F.2d 281 (D. C. Cir. 1948).

¹¹ 321 U.S. 503 (1944).

¹² For example, there is no statutory provision for hearing in deportation cases.

¹³ *Fahey* v. *Mallonee*, 332 U.S. 245 (1947).

¹⁴ *Hagar* v. *Reclamation District*, 111 U.S. 701 (1884); *Phillips* v. *Commissioner*, 283 U.S. 589 (1931).

¹⁵ On rule-making § 4; on adjudication §§ 5, 7, 8, 11.

¹⁶ The APA requires formal procedure in rule-making only where there is a statutory specification that rules are to be made on the basis of a record after the agency affords an opportunity for a hearing. APA § 4 (b).

¹⁷ *American Air Transport* v. *CAB*, 98 F. Supp. 660 (D. D. C. 1951).

¹⁸ A companion case to the *American Air Transport* case (see n. 17), but pertaining to adjudication is *Wong Yang Sung* v. *McGrath* 339 U.S. 33 (1950), where hearing was held to be required in a deportation proceeding.

¹⁹ 308 U.S. 22 (1939).

²⁰ *Report of the Conference on Administrative Procedure Called by the President of the United States*, April 29, 1953; p. 36. See also 2 Davis, *Admin. Law Treatise* § 14.16 (1958), for a discussion of the use of shortened and modified procedure.

²¹ *Report of the Conference on Administrative Procedure* (1953), p. 37. Emphasis supplied.

²² *Ibid.*, pp. 37–38.

²³ *Ibid.*, pp. 71–72.

²⁴ J. D. Bond, "The Use of Pre-Trial Technique in Administrative Hearings," 13 *Journal of the Federal Communications Bar Association*, 55 (1953). Note also 1 Davis *Admin. Law Treatise* § 8.07 (1958).

²⁵ J. D. Bond, *op. cit.* note 24, pp. 56–57.

²⁶ 1923 ICC Annual Rept., pp. 7–8. Emphasis supplied.

²⁷ Attorney General's Committee on Administrative Procedure, monograph, *Interstate Commerce Commission*, Sen. Doc. No. 10, 77th Cong., 1st sess., part 10: p. 23 (1941). (Hereinafter Monograph, ICC).

²⁸ See *Ibid.*, p. 25.

²⁹ *Ibid.*, p. 24.

³⁰ *Ibid.*, p. 25.

³¹ 49 CFR 1.45(a) (1961 Supp.).

³² 49 CFR 1.46(a), 1.47, 1.48, 1.49, 1.50, 1.51, 1.52, 1.54 (1961 Supp.).

³³ 49 CFR 1.53(a) (1961 Supp.).

³⁴ 49 CFR 1.53(b) (1961 Supp.).

³⁵ Anthony F. Arpaia, Hugh W. Cross, Charles D. Mahaffie, Dr. Louis A. Jaffe, Nuel D. Belnap, and John R. Turney (moderator), "A Forum on Improvement of Administrative Procedure," 21 *ICC Practitioners' Journal* 836 (1954).

[36] *Ibid.,* pp. 842–843.

[37] *Ibid.,* p. 838.

[38] The "claim shark" is *one* individual who collects or gathers claims of numerous parties which are attempting to present a collective claim to the Commission. For example, one shark may file a claim on behalf of ninety complainants.

[39] For these arguments see the statement of Nuel D. Belnap, a member of the ICC Bar, in "A Forum on Improvement of Administrative Procedure," 21 *ICC Practitioners' Journal* 843–849, (1954).

[40] Sections 401(c); and 402(e).

[41] Section 1002(d).

[42] Attorney General's Committee on Administrative Procedure, monograph, *Civil Aeronautics Authority,* 77th Cong. 1st sess., Sen. Doc. No. 10, part 6: p. 32 (1941). (Hereinafter Monograph, CAA.)

[43] 1942 CAB Annual Report, p. 23.

[44] 1948 CAB Annual Report, p. 12.

[45] 14 CFR 302.311 (1962 ed.).

[46] 14 CFR 302.312 (1962 ed.).

[47] 14 CFR 302.314 (1962 ed.).

[48] 14 CFR 302.315 (1962 ed.).

[49] 14 CFR 302.316 (1962 ed.).

[50] 14 CFR 302.318 (1962 ed.).

[51] 14 CFR 302.319 (1962 ed.).

[52] 1952 CAB Annual Report, p. 35.

[53] *Ibid.,* p. 35.

[53] Ibid., p. 35.

[54] 1954 CAB Annual Rept., p. 39.

[55] See § 8(b) and § 8(d) of the Securities Act of 1933; §§ 6(e), 19(a)(2), of the Securities Exchange Act of 1934; and §§ 7(b), 10(d), 20(c) of the Holding Company Act of 1935.

[56] Attorney General's Committee on Administrative Procedure, *Securities and Exchange Commission,* Sen. Doc. No. 10, 77th Cong., 1st sess., part 13: p. 31 (1941). (Hereinafter Monograph, SEC.)

[57] *Ibid.,* p. 31.

[58] *Ibid.,* p. 32.

[59] *Ibid.,* p. 58.

[60] A letter sent by the Commission which describes the deficiency of a particular application which does not accord with the law or the rules of the SEC. An opportunity for correction is given by the Commission.

[61] Monograph, SEC, p. 58.

[62] 1947 SEC Annual Rept., p. 35.

[63] *Ibid.,* p. 110.

[64] Monograph, SEC, p. 74.

[65] 17 CFR 202.3(d) (1962 Supp.).

[66] In "A Forum on Improvement of Administrative Procedure," 21 *ICC Practitioners' Journal* 840 (1954)

[67] The use of informal conferences during the course of hearings is similar to the practice of the CAB and the SEC.

[68] 49 CFR 1.68(a) (1961 Supp.).

[69] 49 CFR 1.68(c) (1961 Supp.).

[70] 49 CFR 1.68(d) (1961 Supp.)

[71] See discussion beginning p. 35 herein.

[72] Wilbur La Roe, Jr., "ICC Procedure and Practice," 19 *ICC Practitioners' Journal* 119 (1951). This statement was made before the ICC began to use modified procedure extensively. See above, p. 40, statement of Commissioner Mahaffie. Turney, a prominent ICC practitioner, was a president of the Assoc. of ICC Practitioners.

[73] 17 CFR 201.3(e) (1962 Supp.).

[74] Monograph, SEC, p. 41.

[75] Quoted from an address by Jerome Frank before the Association of the Bar of the City of New York, May 5, 1940; in Monograph, SEC, p. 103.

[76] Monograph, SEC, p. 41.

[77] 14 CFR 302.23 (1962 ed.).

[78] 14 CFR 302.23(b) (1962 ed.).

[79] 14 CFR 302.23(b) (1962 ed.).

[80] 14 CFR 302.22 (1962 ed.).

[81] Monograph, CAA, p. 15.

[82] 1941 CAB Annual Report, p. 7.

[83] Monograph, CAA, fn. 40, p. 16.

[84] CFR 1.111(a) (1958 ed.).

[85] 47 CFR 1.111(a) (1958 ed.).

[86] 47 CFR 1.111(b) (1958 ed.).

[87] 1954 FCC Annual Report, p. 17.

[88] Report of the Committee on Communications, American Bar Association, 6 *Administrative Law Bulletin* 34 (1953).

[89] *Ibid.*, p. 35.

[90] 20 CFR 102.35(g) (1961 Supp.).

[91] 61 Stat. 147 (1947), § 10(c).

[92] Bernard Dunau, "Consent Adjustment Under the National Labor Relations Act," 12 *Federal Bar Journal* 220 (1952).

[93] 16 CFR 3.10 (1960 ed.).

[94] 1918 FTC Annual Rept., pp. 55–56.

[95] Monograph, CAA, p. 38.

[96] Report of the Committee on Communications, American Bar Association, 6 *Administrative Law Bulletin* 35 (1953). Emphasis supplied.

[97] *Ibid.*, p. 36.

[98] APA, § 5.

[99] Kenneth Culp Davis, "The Requirement of Opportunity to be Heard in the Administrative Process," 51 *Yale Law Journal* 1140 (1942).

[100] *Ibid.*, p. 1141.

[101] *Ibid.*, p. 1142.

CHAPTER III: Pp. 02–103

[1] APA, § 5.

[2] APA, § 5(b).

[3] APA, § 10(e)(6).

[4] Ashley Sellers, "'Informal' Dispositions under the Administrative Procedure Act," 32 *American Bar Association Journal* 648 (1946).

[5] "The Federal Administrative Procedure Act Becomes Law, Subcommittee Chairman Walter's Statement," 32 *ABAJ.* 377, at 386 (1946).

[6] Sellers, *op. cit.* note 4, p. 648.

[7] 48 Stat. 74.

[8] 48 Stat. 881.
[9] 49 Stat. 803.
[10] 53 Stat. 1149.
[11] 54 Stat. 789.
[12] 54 Stat. 847.
[13] Monograph, SEC, *op. cit.* chap. ii, n. 56: pp. 7–8.
[14] 17 CFR 202.1(c) (1962 Supp.).
[15] 17 CFR 202.1(d) (1962 Supp.).
[16] 17 CFR 202.2 (1962 Supp.).
[17] 17 CFR 202.3(b) (1962 Supp.).
[18] 17 CFR 202.4(b) (1961 Supp.).
[19] In such a case informal techniques should be considered as shortened procedure, in the sense discussed in chapter ii.
[20] 1935 SEC Annual Rept., p. 9.
[21] *Ibid.,* p. 10.
[22] *Ibid.*
[23] Monograph, SEC, p. 16.
[24] *Ibid.,* p. 18, n. 39.
[25] *Ibid.*
[26] *Ibid.*
[27] 17 CFR 202.3(a) (1962 Supp.).
[28] 1951 SEC Annual Rept., p. 2.
[29] *Ibid.,* pp. 2–3.
[30] 1951 SEC Annual Rept., p. 3.
[31] Monograph SEC, p. 24.
[32] *Ibid.*
[33] *Ibid.*
[34] Monograph, SEC, p. 26. Emphasis supplied.
[35] Section 15(b).
[36] James M. Landis, *The Administrative Process* (New Haven: Yale University Press, 1938), pp. 109–110.
[37] *Ibid.,* p. 110.
[38] 1951 SEC Annual Report, pp. 15–16.
[39] 1961 SEC Annual Report, p. 261.
[40] *Ibid.,* p. 259.
[41] Monograph, ICC, *op. cit.* chap. ii, n. 27, p. 72.
[42] Monograph, ICC, p. 73.
[43] Letter to the author, Aug. 16, 1957, from Robert J. Test, Acting Secretary of the Interstate Commerce Commission.
[44] 49 CFR 1.200(a) (1961 Supp.).
[45] Monograph, ICC, p. 50.
[46] Letter to the author, *op. cit.* note 43.
[47] *Ibid.*
[48] Letter to the author, *op. cit.* note 43.
[49] *Ibid.*
[50] 49 CFR 1.200(a) (1961 Supp.).
[51] U.S., Congress, House, Select Committee to investigate the FCC, *Final Rept.,* 80th Cong., 2nd Sess., 1949, H. Rept. 2479. With respect to the telephone industry, in 1959 its gross investment was 24 billion dollars, and its annual revenues over $8 billion. 1959 FCC Annual Report, p. 6.
[52] 1959 FCC Annual Report, p. 1.
[53] All these figures are in 1961 FCC Annual Report, pp. 18–19.

[54] 47 CFR 1.301 (1958 ed.).

[55] 47 CFR 1.321 (1958 ed.).

[56] 47 CFR 1.341; 1.342; 1.343 (1958 ed.).

[57] 47 CFR 1.361 (1961 Supp.).

[58] 47 CFR 1.447 (1958 ed.).

[59] 47 CFR 1.372(a) (1956 Supp.).

[60] 47 CFR 1.372(b) (1956 Supp.).

[61] 47 CFR 1.372(c) (1956 Supp.).

[62] 47 CFR 1.361 (1961 Supp.).

[63] 47 CFR 1.363; 1.364 (1958 ed.).

[64] 47 CFR 1.361 (1961 Supp.).

[65] 47 CFR 1.355(d) (1958 ed.).

[66] 47 CFR 1.364(a)(b) (1958 ed.).

[67] 47 CFR 1.78 (1961 Supp.).

[68] 47 CFR 1.63 and 1.72 (1958 ed.) respectively.

[69] Attorney General's Committee on Administrative Procedure, Monograph, *Federal Communications Commission,* Sen. Doc. No. 186, 76th Cong. 3rd Sess., part 3: p. 43 (1940). (Hereinafter, Monograph, FCC.)

[70] *Ibid.*

[71] Compare *Ibid.*, pp. 50–51 with 47 CFR 1.72 (1958 ed.).

[72] Monograph, FCC, p. 51.

[73] Monograph, FCC, p. 52.

[74] U.S., House, Antitrust Subcommittee of the Committee on the Judiciary, *Hearings, Monopoly Problems in Regulated Industries,* 84th Congress, 2nd Sess., 1957, part 2, vol. 1, pp. 3228–3230. Emphasis supplied.

[75] *Ibid.*, p. 3157. From FCC Report No. 2793, Broadcast Actions.

[76] *Ibid.*, p. 3159.

[77] See, for example, 1959 FCC Annual Rept., p. 109.

[78] Monograph, FCC, p. 54.

[79] 49 Stat. 449, § 9 (1935).

[80] *Ibid.*, § 9(b).

[81] 61 Stat. 136 (1957).

[82] 1948 NLRB Annual Rept., p. 41.

[83] Attorney General's Committee on Administrative Procedure, monograph, *National Labor Relations Board,* Sen. Doc. No. 10, 77th Cong., 1st Sess., part 5: p. 32 (1941).

[84] 61 Stat. 136 (1947).

[85] 29 CFR 101.19. (1961 Supp.).

[86] Bernard Dunau, "Consent Adjustment Under the National Labor Relatons Act," 12 *Federal Bar Journal* 216–217 (1952).

[87] A hearing may or may not be held. 29 CFR 101.19(b) (1961 Supp.).

[88] Dunau, *op. cit.* note 86, p. 217.

[89] *Ibid.*

[90] 29 CFR 101.19(a)(5) (1961 Supp.).

[91] 29 CFR 101.19(a) (1961 Supp.).

[92] Dunau, *op. cit.*, p. 218.

CHAPTER IV: Pp. 104–144

[1] 1953 Annual Rept. of the Commissioner of Internal Revenue, p. 22.

[2] U.S. Treasury Dept., Office of the Commissioner of Internal Revenue,

IR-Mimeograph No. 6, Reo. No. 6; Aud. No. 2. Contained in *The Internal Revenue Service, Its Reorganzation and Administration,* U.S. Cong., Joint Committee on Internal Revenue Taxation (Wash., 1955).

[3] *Ibid.,* n. 31.

[4] Rev. Proc. 56–34, *Internal Revenue Bulletin* 1956–45, p. 32, § 6.03.

[5] IR-Mimeograph No. 6, *op. cit.* note 2.

[6] *The Internal Revenue Service, Its Reorganization and Administration, op. cit.* note 2 (Wash., 1955), p. 8.

[7] *Ibid.,* p. 9.

[8] The figures for 1952 are used, for at that time a contested case was the same as a protested case.

[9] This assumes a relatively constant ratio between the number of cases involving deficiencies and the number in which the taxpayers decided to contest in 1952 and 1954. The interpolation is based upon the ratios for these years. By 1954 the initial period of adjustment with respect to the use of the new procedure would have ended. In 1952, 6.9 per cent of the total number of deficiencies were protested and contested. This involved all preappellate cases *and* cases filed with the Appellate Division. In 1954, protested cases involved *only* cases filed with the Appellate Division. If a constant ratio between deficiencies and contested cases is assumed, the reduction in the number of cases "protested" between 1952 and 1954 represents the number of *contested* cases settled at the preappellate stage.

[10] U.S. Congress, House, Special Subcommittee on Legislative Oversight, Committee on Interstate and Foreign Commerce, *Independent Regulatory Commissions,* H. Rept. No. 2711, 85th Cong., 2nd Sess., 1959, p. 50.

[11] 1916 FTC Annual Rept., p. 8.

[12] 1926 FTC Annual Rept., p. 4.

[13] 38 Stat. 717 (1914).

[14] Rule III, FTC Rules of Practice, 1927; in 1927 FTC Annual Rept., pp. 126–127. Emphasis suppled.

[15] Letter to the author.

[16] 1951 FTC Annual Rept., p. 82.

[17] 61 Stat. 149, § 10(k) (1947).

[18] Information concerning the early operation of the Board may be found in the Attorney General's Committee on Administrative Procedure monograph, National Labor Relations Board, Sen. Doc. No. 10, 77 Cong., 1st Sess., part 5 (1941).

[19] 1960 NLRB Annual Rept., p. 13.

[20] This information has been gained from NLRB statistics contained in its Annual Reports.

[21] 1936 NLRB Annual Rept., p. 31.

[22] See, for example, *Poole Foundry and Machine Co.* v. *NLRB,* 192 F. 2d 740 (1951); *NLRB* v. *Newspaper and Mail Deliverers' Union,* 192 F. 2d 654 (1951); and *NLRB* v. *J. L. Hudson Co.,* 135 F. 2d 380 (1943); *Wallace Corp.* v. *NLRB,* 323 U.S. 248 (1944).

[23] The Rules of Practice of the ICC are contained in 49 CFR 1961 Supp.

[24] O. L. Mohundro, "Improvements in Procedure before the Commission," 20 *ICC Practitioners' Journal* 77 (1952).

[25] Letter to the author from Robert J. Test, Acting Secretary of the Interstate Commerce Commission, Aug. 16, 1957.

[26] 24 Stat. 379 (1887), § 1.

[27] Letter to the author, *op. cit.* n. 25.

²⁸ 1960 ICC Annual Rept., p. 108.
²⁹ For example, Commission on Organization of the Executive Branch of the Government, *Task Force Report on Regulatory Commissions,* Appendix N (Washington, 1949).
³⁰ 1960 SEC Annual Rept., p. 201.
³¹ 1951 SEC Annual Rept., p. 154.
³² 1960 SEC Annual Rept., p. 200.
³³ *Ibid.,* p. 201.
³⁴ 48 Stat. 1064, § 3(h) (1934).
³⁵ *Wall Street Journal,* June 29, 1961, p. 1.
³⁶ The figures for 1947, 1948, and 1950 are contained in the Annual Reports of the CAB. The figures for 1959 are contained n the 1959 Annual Rept. of the Office of Administrative Procedure, p. 39.
³⁷ 1959 CAB Annual Rept., p. 33.
³⁸ 1959 Annual Rept. of the Office of Administrative Procedure, p. 39.

CHAPTER V: Pp. 145–165

¹ The term "pure administrative process" is derived from Walter Gellhorn and Clark Byse, *Administrative Law: Cases and Comments* (Brooklyn: The Foundation Press, 1960), p. 657.
² These figures are contained in the 1960 VA Annual Rept.
³ 1958–1959 United States Government Organization Manual, p. 511.
⁴ 1956 VA Annual Rept., p. 117. Emphasis supplied.
⁵ All information concerning the work of the VA in fiscal 1960 is contained in the Annual Report for that year.
⁶ The procedural regulations of the Veterans Administration are contained in 38 CFR 1961 Supp.
⁷ 48 Stat. 9 (1934).
⁸ *Silberschein* v. *U.S.,* 266 U.S. 221 (1924); *Lynch* v. *U.S.,* 292 U.S. 571 (1933); *Meadows* v. *U.S.,* 281 U.S. 271 (1930); *U.S.* v. *Hines,* 13 F. 2d 514 (App. D. C., 1934). Recent cases include *Thompson* v. *Whittier,* 185 F. Supp. 306 (D.D.C. 1960).
⁹ 1960 VA Annual Rept., p. 105.
¹⁰ Ralph Gower, "Fact Finding in the Field Office," 7 *Social Security Bulletin* No. 1, p. 32 (1944).
¹¹ *Ibid.,* pp. 32–33.
¹² Victor Christgau, "Old-Age and Survivors Insurance After Twenty Years," 18 *Social Security Bulletin* No. 8, p. 15 (1955).
¹³ *Ibid.,* pp. 15–16.
¹⁴ Information concerning the early operation of the BOASI in the disability field is contained in Arthur Hess, "Old-Age, Survivors, and Disability Insurance: Early Problems and Operations of the Disability Provisions," 20 *Social Security Bulletin* No. 12 (1957).
¹⁵ The procedural rules of the BOASI are contained in 20 CFR 1961 ed.
¹⁶ Information concerning the establishment of an appellate system for the BOASI may be found in Attorney General's Committee on Administrative Procedure, monograph, Social Security Board, Sen. Doc. No. 10, 77th Cong., 1st Sess., part 3 (1941).
¹⁷ *Ibid.,* pp. 45–46.

[18] 1960 FCC Annual Rept., p. 115.
[19] *Ibid.,* p. 116.
[20] 1960 ICC Annual Rept., p. 127.
[21] *Ibid.,* p. 130.

CHAPTER VI: Pp. 166–190

[1] See Commission on Organization of the Executive Branch of the Government, *Task Force Rept. on Legal Services and Procedure* (Wash., 1955).
[2] All preceding quotations by the task force are in *Ibid.,* p. 138.
[3] *Ibid.,* p. 139.
[4] U.S., Congress, Senate, Subcommittee on Administrative Practice and Procedure of the Committee on the Judiciary, *Hearings, Federal Administrative Procedure,* 86th Cong., 2nd Sess., 1960, pp. 65–66.
[5] *Ibid.,* p. 79. See also S. 1887, 87th Cong., 1st Sess. (1961).
[6] *Federal Administrative Procedure, op. cit.* note 4, p. 237. Emphasis supplied.
[7] *Ibid.,* p. 238–239.
[8] *Ibid.,* pp. 231–232.
[9] This summary of management firm reports on the regulatory agencies was written by the Bureau of the Budget, and is contained in *Ibid.,* pp. 40–41.
[10] James M. Landis, *Report on Regulatory Agencies to the President-Elect,* submitted by the Chairman of the Subcommittee on Adminstrative Practice and Procedure to the Committee on the Judiciary of the United States Senate, 86th Cong., 2nd Sess., Dec., 1960 (committee print).
[11] The courts can always intervene in administrative proceedings, regardless of congressional preclusion of review; however, they generally will not do so where expert considerations are determinative to administrative judgment. Where the rights of individuals are involved, and where protection is considered inadequate, the courts may invoke the Constitution to exercise judicial review. The power of Congress is great, as is indicated in the aftermath of *Wong Yang Sung v. McGrath,* 339 U.S. 33 (1950), where Congress excluded immigration proceedings from the requirements of the Administrative Procedure Act after the Court had held that the APA requirements should be followed in such proceedings to conform to *constitutional* standards of due process. In this case, Congress in effect overruled the Supreme Court.
[12] Several articles illustrative of this point are J. P. Harris, "The Senatorial Rejection of Leland Olds," 35 *American Pol. Science Rev.* 647–693 (1951); and S. Huntington, "The Marasmus of the ICC," 61 *Yale Law Journal* 467–509.
[13] Report of the Committee on Ministers' Powers, Cmd. 4060, April, 1932.
[14] *Ibid.,* p. 76.
[15] *Ibid.,* pp. 79–80.
[16] See particularly APA §§ 7–10.
[17] James M. Landis, *The Administrative Process* (New Haven: Yale University Press, 1938), p. 38.
[18] *Ibid.,* p. 39.

Index

Acceleration, of registration statements by the SEC, 72–74, 80

Administrative adjudication: definition of, 2; importance of, 2; and the common law, 10–16; development of informal procedure, 24–30; and traditional legal procedure, 166, 167–170; reforms proposed, 167–177; reforms evaluated, 177–190; criteria for, 182–186

Administrative courts, 17–18

Administrative law, legal criticism of, 166, 167–170

Administrative Procedure Act, 20–21, 33–34, 59, 62–65, 181

Administrative process, development of, 5

Administrative sanctions, and the SEC, 137

American Bar Association: diversity within, 16–17; and the development of administrative agencies, 16–21; attitude toward prehearing procedure, 55, 57–59; criticisms of administrative procedure, 168–170; proposals for reform of administrative procedure, 167, 171–172; evaluation of reform proposals, 177–190

Application cases: definition of, 62; nature and importance of, 62, 101–103; and the SEC, 65–80; ICC, 80–87; FCC, 87–96; NLRB, 97–101

Assigned Car Cases (1927), 32–33

Attorney General's Committee on Administrative Procedure, 25, 30; and the CAB, 43, 53, 57; SEC, 47–48, 51, 66, 69, 70; ICC, 81, 83; FCC, 91, 95; NLRB, 97–98

Bi-Metallic Co. v. Colorado (1915), 32

Bowles v. Willingham (1944), 33

Bureau of Old-Age and Survivors Insurance, 3, 152–160

Bureau of the Budget, management surveys on administrative agencies, 173–174

Civil Aeronautics Board, 3; use of shortened procedure, 43–46; prehearing procedure, 52–53; requirement for hearings, 59, 102; complaint cases, 140–142; and the pure administrative process, 163–164

Coke (Edward), 10

Committee on Ministers' Powers (Great Britain), 183

Common law, contrasted with administrative law, 10–16

Complaint cases: definition, 104; nature and importance of, 104, 142–144; and the IRS, 104–116; FTC, 116–124; NLRB, 125–129; ICC, 129–134; SEC, 134–138; FCC, 138–140; CAB, 140–142

Conference on Administrative Procedure, 35–36

Constitution of the United States: separation of powers, 1; administrative branch, 1–2; and the development of administrative law, 8–10; providing context of administrative action, 179–182

Contact personnel, and the VA, 147–148

Courts, deficiencies of, 5–7

Davis (Kenneth Culp), 25, 60–61

Deficiency letters, and the SEC, 71–72, 79–80

Demurrage disputes, and the ICC, 133

Dicey (A. V.), 10–11, 16

Dickinson (John), 2, 15 16

Droit administratif, 11

Due process of law, and administrative proceedings, 21–24

Federal Aviation Agency, 163–164

Federal Communications Commission: 3; prehearing procedure, 53–55, 57–59; requirement for hearings, 59; application cases,

201